getting into the act

getting into the act

*Opening Up Lay Ministry in the Weekday World

FREDERICK K. WENTZ

ABINGDON
NASHVILLE

GETTING INTO THE ACT

Copyright © 1978 by Abingdon

Library of Congress Cataloging in Publication Data

WENTZ, FREDERICK K
  Getting into the act.
  1. Christian life—Lutheran authors. 2. Laity. 3. Liberation
theology. I. Title.
BV4501.2.W4198   248'.48'41   78-17179

ISBN 0-687-14125-7

Scripture quotations are from the Revised Standard
Common Bible, copyrighted © 1973.

Photograph on page 136 is used by permission of the
Maryknoll Fathers, Maryknoll, New York. Copyright © 1970.

The poetry on pages 139 and 140, from *The Desert Is Fertile*
by Dom Helder Camara, is reprinted by permission of Orbis
Books and of Sheed and Ward, Ltd., publishers.

MANUFACTURED BY THE PARTHENON PRESS AT
NASHVILLE, TENNESSEE, UNITED STATES OF AMERICA

To our son Ted (1953–1975)
who in brief years here
made good beginnings toward
a simpler, freer way of life

Contents

Preface

The important action in our world is God's action. What is God doing here and now? Christians have the best clue by noting what God has been doing in Jesus Christ, reconciling human beings to himself.

Maybe you are an amateur actor. A great play comes to your city and you don't want to miss it. You compete to get the best ticket at the right price. You fight traffic, pay an exorbitant parking fee, and push through crowds to your seat. You settle back to be entertained. You are absorbed in the beginning lines when the play suddenly takes a startling turn: spotlights focus on you, and the leading actor beckons you forward to take your place in the dramatic action! You are surprised and afraid and thoroughly involved. It could be an opportunity. Surely, He knows what He is doing. Both hesitant and confident, you move forward, all unprepared, and get into the action.

So it is when the gospel of Jesus Christ takes hold of you. So it is when you respond by moving forward into God's modern world.

What is the main thrust of God's action in the modern world?

The best sign of his reconciliation, around the world, is more people wanting to get into the action. Today there are increasing numbers of those who stand up to be counted as responsible human beings, who want to participate in the decisions affecting their personal lives, their communities, their nations, and their globe. God's hand is in this modern movement.

What is the main ministry of the church within that action?

Its surest sign is people involved in God's liberating thrust in the name of Jesus Christ, actively ministering within the struggles of all these human beings for freedom, mature fulfillment, and justice.

How can laity best get into the act?

Lay people are part of the action when they think and respond in their daily routines and decisions as part of the church's liberating ministry. Ministry, so defined, belongs to all the baptized People of God. All of us are beckoned into the act.

Granted, it's not quite that simple. The devil and human sin foul up God's action in the modern world. In fact, it's not simple at all to find the Christian way in today's life; but, clearly, it does mean getting into the act.

getting
into
the
act

Chapter One

We're Ordinary People Not Heroes

The world is too big for most of us, and there are too many things wrong with it. But we want to do our little part to improve things. We want to help people. So we pick out a few causes; we give some money; maybe we write a letter or two to members of congress; we may even give time and energy as local leaders.

For example, I belong to Common Cause. I believe in its purposes; I pay for an annual membership; I read some of the literature; once in a while I write a letter. I have about the same level of participation in Bread for the World. Someday, I tell myself, I'm going to get more deeply involved. Meanwhile, I take mild satisfaction in knowing that activist people are making a dent in some pressing problems by building upon myself and many others as a base of support. I'm not among the astronauts, but I put in a few licks as part of the ground crew or support team.

Can it be said that I do this as an essential part of my response to the gospel of Jesus Christ? Most sermons use more heroic examples, like Dag Hammarskjöld or Martin Luther King, Jr. or Dom Helder Camara, Archbishop of Recife in Brazil.

One thesis of this book is that great public servants, genuine modern liberators, need help from many of us ordinary people.

We provide the supply trains for "far-out" liberators. And that is no petty or insignificant Christian service, or ministry.

Nor is it easy to provide supply trains. Two recent personal experiences will illustrate the issues with which this book deals. The first describes the ministry of a priest I met in Argentina several years ago.

He tells a simple story, this pastor with a parish of twelve thousand people scattered widely over a rural area. But there is real excitement among them. The pastor says it's because he preaches God's Word. Here's what he tells them:

From the two central events in the Bible—the deliverance of the Israelites from Egypt and Jesus' ministry to men and women—each Christian's life story takes its shape. These two events shape the story of all humankind as well. First, the children of Israel were half-miserable and half-content as slaves in Egypt. God intervened and called them out into the desert. There they suffered and complained but eventually became a free people under God. The second event is Jesus' calling his contemporaries from oppression and blind acceptance into freedom and a new awareness of the fullness of life.

For the Argentine pastor the central symbols are the Passover and Easter. But the cross is central too, and none of this liberation comes without suffering, without reluctance, without resistance. Still, he preaches freedom and the people respond enthusiastically.

Simple, isn't it? And it's great!

Of course, I should add that this priest's people are very poor; they feel oppressed and boxed in. When he preaches freedom, they enthusiastically start to seek justice in their jobs and in their politics. That is where they know they want freedom. But that causes trouble almost instantly. Therefore, when Father Escos talks about the cross he knows he's talking about violence.

Furthermore, the Argentine government does not tolerate resistance. I was not surprised, the day after meeting this priest, to read in the paper about the arrest of some of his like-minded colleagues in a nearby city.

What's wrong with this picture? When I describe it to some of my North American friends they feel there's a confusion here—one shouldn't use Bible stories politically. But Father Escos claims he just preaches the stories straight. And they *are* political stories. Isn't it entirely possible that the direct telling of the good news is dynamite?

What shall we do about socially radical applications of the gospel? Can we support freedom movements for the poor and the oppressed? What if violence results from a group's actions? Do we want to provide supply trains for such people and their thrusts toward freedom?

My second experience, also from several years ago, involves Elliott Couden, a Protestant layman from Seattle. At a lay conference I was in a group of frustrated people for whom there were not enough hotel rooms. I bid on a room at the same time as a stranger; it was a double room, and we became roommates. When I heard his story I got him to write a chapter for a book I was editing. The book was called *My Job and My Faith,* and his chapter was titled "The Supply Trains Are Missing." He had his own real estate business in Seattle and was the first realtor in that city to commit himself and his business to integrated housing. All hell broke loose. He stuck it out, but he felt badly let down by the churches, despite some ministerial support. He explains his experience under this metaphor:

> It was as if a layman, encouraged to plant the symbol of the faith on top a snow-capped mountain, found himself there surrounded with lonely, howling winds with no supply trains, little or no communication and a slim chance ever to return to the home base. I am not unhappy with any particular church for this deficiency. I am just aghast at the way the church prepares and supports its soldiers in battle![1]

15

Hendrik Kraemer has suggested that telling a layperson to go into the modern world and live a Christian life is like telling that person to go alone and unprepared to live at the North Pole. What we need most of all is supply trains that reach lay people in their outposts within the weekday world. What's wrong with the modern church that it cannot stand behind its lay leaders, those who pioneer for freedom and justice? And what can be done to overcome this glaring weakness in the church's life? In chapter 4 these questions are addressed under the heading "Where Are the Supply Trains?"

In all, then, this chapter poses three kinds of questions for the reader and for the rest of this volume: (1) How does the ordinary Christian relate to the more strenuous or far-out agents of social change? (2) How does the gospel relate to radical movements for social change? (3) How does the church in its present forms help or hinder these two relationships?

First let's turn, in the next chapter, to the controlling image for this volume: freedom/liberation.

Chapter Two

Liberation:
Who Needs It?

Freedom: Who Needs It?

As recently as seventy-five years ago these words were, for the bulk of Americans, a genuine and pressing question. The phrase could have been the slogan for our early, great crusade. Freedom: we had it, and we wanted to export it for the good of the world.

We had received the ideal of freedom through a long and honored tradition: from ancient Greece, the Bible, the carriers of Western civilization, the Protestant Reformation, the Enlightenment, the Declaration of Independence. Now we Americans actually had it. This nation, "conceived in liberty," as Lincoln put it, was the great experiment in freedom and democracy. And it was highly successful. So, naturally, we exported it.

Who needs freedom? Here we come, the liberators. Here we come with advice about political forms, with an American version of the gospel, with gunboats and military intelligence, with salespeople and investors. We spread our protecting arms over Latin Americans so that they would get their freedom only from us.

But that was seventy-five years ago. Today the crusade is long gone. For many middle-class white American Protestants that slogan could only be cynically said, with a shrug of the shoulders: Freedom, who needs it?

We have failed to export freedom. We don't know how. The proof was in Vietnam. There we saw our outreach at its worst. However much many of us may have wanted freedom and democracy for the Vietnamese, our efforts were reduced to helping those people survive our own destructive force.

Yet, here's the real paradox. Just as we are disillusioned about the spread of freedom—even about world missions and the spread of Christian freedom—the world is experiencing a great surge in the desire of peoples to be free.

Our politicians in recent political campaigns did not talk of spreading freedom. Rather, they talked as though, since we are free—we mainline majority Americans—the issues are energy shortages, peace in the Middle East, unemployment, inflation, reorganized welfare, and (always) taxes. They talked that way because so many Americans feel that way—as though freedom were a past achievement, something we got in 1776. Or as though the voices of dissent peaked in 1968 when the Blacks and the youth had their say.

The terrible irony is, I repeat, that increasing millions of humanity all around us on this globe are both yearning for and alert to the revolution that is coming soon. It will bring them, they believe, real freedom. We live now in an age of revolution, and the immediate future will be an age of revolution. All kinds of revolutions. But the major goal is freedom.

The basic revolution is one of *rising expectations* here, there, and everywhere around the globe. It rides the wheels of technology. Today the oppressed and the poor see in technology the power to control nature, and to control one's own destiny. That's what freedom is—the power to control one's own destiny. The power-hungry poor of our earth see in technology the possibility of *human dignity.*

Millions of earth's creatures are rising from the mire of

superstition or the chains of dominance by their fellow creatures and are declaring: *We too are human.* Away with the peasant mentality—arms in front of the face to fend off blows of an uncertain providence or the beatings of one's superiors. Away with the slave mentality! There must be an end to the coolie approach to life, the colonial outlook. Throughout the world there are rising expectations of all kinds, but the central cry is for liberation.

If there is any progress to be seen among people in this twentieth century, other than the increase of technology, it is the biblical prospect of the increase of both good and evil possibilities, the wheat and the tares that both grow until the end. There is a startling increase of people who want to get into the act, who want to say yes or no for themselves. They want to act in history, not just be acted upon. They intend to help shape their own destinies. They expect to stand up and be counted. God is doing that on this planet during these decades. No matter how we like it.

So what do we do with this huge freedom movement? Where does freedom fit for us? How do Americans, how do Christians fit in with this liberation groundswell?

One more fact must be added, a fact which heightens the problem for Americans faltering in their commitment to freedom just when many others are reaching strenuously for that very item. From our perspective, the world is full of surging, seething minorities with which we must deal; we know we are awkward about it. But many people in the Third World see us mainline Americans as the real, sticky minority problem in the world today. If the issue is the redistribution of power so that people everywhere can make decisions with dignity, then, from the world's viewpoint, the worst minority problem is the white, the Westerner, the middle class, the North American, the power elite in industry, education, wealth, and military hardware. This is a gross oversimplification, to which exception can easily be made, but it carries its penetrating truth as well.

Some years ago I was in Panama City talking with some Panamanians about Christian missions. At the end, these young people pulled in another topic. "That hill," they said, pointing to the feature that dominated the city scene through the hotel window, "is now owned by the United States. Tell your people back home that we want our sovereignty." For me that incident symbolized not only the feelings of two million Panamanians but also the anguish, pride, and search for dignity of hosts of Third World people.

Freedom and Liberation

It's not that we're opposed to freedom. Everybody believes that freedom is a good thing, properly interpreted, of course. It's that we are very unsure about liberation.

Freedom is a long-recognized American ideal, stemming from the ideas of the Enlightenment that shaped the beginnings of this nation. Liberation implies revolution and often sounds foreign, as though it belongs to Marxists. Freedom can be thought of primarily in individual terms, whereas liberation implies social movement. Freedom fits with past accomplishments and established rights. Liberation involves change and the overcoming of oppression.

But for many of us the main problem with the idea of liberation is that it implies rapid change. Liberation means freeing people who have been bound by or dependent upon other people. To propose such action makes those other people very uneasy. What things of importance to me will get smashed in the liberation process? Will the freeing of women mean a loss for men? Will freedom for black Africans threaten international economic stability? Will liberation destroy the ordered patterns of our society? What will replace our present order? Typically,

Americans will ask that would-be liberators provide a plan for the future society that can be proved superior—for these same Americans—to the present arrangements.

Liberators can't do that. That's not humanly possible. For that reason, only slaves, who know they are miserable, will move out into the desert from Pharaoh's city on the strength of vague projections of a promised land.

Well, there is one other group—those with a strong sense of calling. Abraham went out from a pleasant and settled existence in Ur, "not knowing where he was to go," because God called him. The typical American doesn't have that sense of calling today.

What about Christians? Does their commitment to freedom include calling? If so, then that's all it takes to make freedom-lovers into liberators.

What does freedom mean for Christians? A common-sense, dictionary definition of freedom speaks of exemption from external control and the power to determine one's own action. But the matter is more complex and goes deeper than that. One theologian calls freedom "that act including most of our being in major decisions or crises and the subsequent responses flowing from it." Thus, freedom is connected with the depth of personhood. If a whole person is a deep well, true freedom is an ingredient at the source that colors and flavors the whole thing. Freedom is giving yourself to what is deepest within you and staying with it in the rest of your responses.

Thus freedom lies in the wisest and deepest self-commitment to whatever one considers most basic. Freedom arises from love or loyalty. One may make a choice, consciously or unconsciously. But then there is an involvement that binds one's roots firmly to the soil so that one may find sustenance there, in order that the rest of the person is free to grow toward the sky. For the Christian that means commitment to the God known in Christ Jesus, and it includes a calling.

Specifically, the Christian has a threefold perspective on freedom: *God created us,* including freedom; *we sinned,* and twisted or defaced ourselves and our freedom; *through Christ we are reconstituted* and given renewed freedom. In other words, human beings are made with the possibility for freedom as a gift. We also receive the task of actualizing our own freedom and the freedom of others, through the power of the Holy Spirit. We are set free in order to serve. Our freedom lies in commitment to God and to the tasks God gives us.

Therefore, we can confidently assert that Christians are called to be free, and to become liberators in Christ's name.

This can mean some very radical commitments to change and to a new order of life, a new society. What does it mean for American church people today? Let me make three ground-rule statements and draw a conclusion.

The first is that we live with an "eschatological itch." We believe that when human history boils down to its basics or comes to its Last Things (the Eschaton), there will be transformation without destroying all continuity. This new society will be shaped by God and will reflect his purposes, so that Christians now live in longing for that day. This longing or itch affects everything we do today, and sometimes it shows up in specific actions and attitudes. We not only long for it, we work for that day!

The second ground rule is this: God's calling and that itch for change will come in a different form for different Christians, according to circumstances, previous commitments, and personal temperament. The star of Bethlehem led the wise men on a long journey with rich gifts. The same event, no doubt with similar transforming power, caught the shepherds in a vision at their daily work, to which they likely returned after seeing the Christ Child.

Some Christians are called into heroic and public leadership—like Elliott Couden in race relations in Seattle—while others are called into new attitudes and a different way of voting and chatting, and into quiet efforts to change the directions of their friends, congregations, and voluntary organizations. Some Christians are called to leave their country and kin for overseas missionary work. Many more are called to support the overseas work—with gifts and prayers and knowledge—while carrying through missionary (evangelistic) responsibilities within a particular American neighborhood.

Similarly, there are far-out Christians who are personally and deeply involved in radical liberation movements, probably finding themselves in conflict with some of the establishments in American society. Other Christians remain within established systems, experiencing less tension, less eschatological itch. They try to improve life but may have more "holy patience," whereas the far-out ones evidence "holy impatience." The second group is more difficult to distinguish from the nominal Christians or the non–Christians in our society. That does not mean that they are less dedicated or called than the far-out ones.

One way to distinguish this second group, however, is to note their concern for the far-out ones, their genuine support for the serious liberation movements that mark the modern world. That's the third ground rule. You may carry out your days in fairly traditional ways within the established institutions of American society. But, if you are responding to God's call for human liberation in the closing decades of the twentieth century, you will be throwing your weight—in small ways or in large ones—in favor of change toward justice and freedom for all people. You may do no more than vote, or you may be quite politically active; your gifts may be small or large; your prayers may or may not be eloquent, fervent, or constant; your lifestyle may change moderately, or it may take a drastic turn. But your commitment is on the side of greater freedom.

My conclusion is this: You are probably not the astronaut, but you belong on the team as part of the ground crew, the communication system, or those who provide backup services. You may not be on the front line of guerilla warfare, but you are committed to keeping the supplies rolling to the front. You're not the climber who will reach the highest peak, but you are an essential part of the whole enterprise, because you are part of the supply train. Your vote, your money, your muscle, your prayer, your expressed attitudes, and your lifestyle provide the essential resources without which far-out liberators will die. That makes you a liberator too. You are getting into God's act and helping others to get into that act.

How the Rest of the Book Goes

Is this a disturbing way to think? There certainly are problems involved in a commitment to social change today. Succeeding chapters will address some of the troubling questions raised by the assertion that you are a liberator.

Chapter 3 asks about the church's role in the modern world. In much of history the church has been a major force for stability and for resisting change. Without doubt, part of the church's function is to conserve and to preserve the good features and constructive values of any society. But essentially the church, according to the New Testament, is an agency for change, comprised of people caught up in a movement with goals beyond their immediate societies. The New Testament word for church is *ecclesia,* which means "called out." Abraham is the forefather for all Christians, both because he lived by faith and because he answered God's call to go out from settled ways into a tenting and nomadic existence as a carrier of God's meaning for all humankind. Events in the twentieth century have conspired to bring this truth forcefully to the attention of the modern church.

Chapter 4 asks how this new situation and changed role affects life in a congregation or parish. Elliott Couden's cry is analyzed and some suggestions are offered for new ways of thinking and organizing within parishes and the church at large.

Chapter 5 discusses the main outlines of Liberation Theology—South American style—and relates them to the Reformation theology that continues to undergird much of traditional church life in America.

Chapter 6 asks how Christians go about making basic decisions in the complexities of modern life while committed to liberation. Clearly, not every modern trend or group that claims to be liberating deserves the support of Christians. Christians won't even agree as they seek to be discriminating. How does one decide?

Chapter 7 asks the same question, both in terms of lifestyle and on the larger scale of the whole church's contribution to the broad sweep of modern society. While the church always has as its central task the reconciliation of all humankind with God, How do we shape our lifestyles for effective service today? and What are the specific and crying needs of people in our generation to which a servant church should address itself?

The final chapter speaks of images and how they shape both life and thought, concluding with a brief picture of Dom Helder Camara.

Chapter Three

The Church as Liberated Minority

The End of Christendom

The most significant event in the life of the Christian church in this twentieth century is the *end of Christendom.* We are still engaged in a severe struggle in America to overcome the *idea* of Christendom.

For centuries it was a noble idea—that all the people of a given territory could be baptized and practicing Christians so that their thinking, customs, laws, and institutions would constitute a Christian civilization, a society shaped by the Christian church and serving as a vehicle for conveying the gospel. For centuries this idea found partial embodiment in a particular piece of geography, medieval Europe, and in the lands and peoples subsequently dominated by European nations, right through the imperialistic nineteenth century.

Actually, since the fourth century (the time of Constantine and Theodosius), and since the ninth century (the time of Charlemagne and the Holy Roman Empire) people have talked about two conjoint works of God, namely, church and state. In many ways the church was in those days, and for many centuries thereafter, the actual carrier of the civilization. The church dominated the state at times and often was the unifying force within the civilization. From this standpoint the Reformation was a setback, a reversion to a degree of tribalism. But in 1917 the Bolsheviks arose in Russia, which had been considered a Christian land. Then in 1933 the Nazis emerged in Germany, which had been considered the heartland of Protestantism and had also been a stronghold of Roman Catholicism. Thus Christendom ceased to be a meaningful term.

Surely, then, Christendom is gone. The intimate relation between the Christian church and the leading forces of Western civilization is at an end. Space-occupying, culture-dominating Christianity has had its day. This fact is hard for Americans to grasp because our patterns of life and mind-set have changed less from the nineteenth to the late twentieth century than those of almost any other civilized people.

This obsolete "fortress" mentality was well illustrated for me when Madalyn Murray O'Hair, noted opponent of the churches, was invited to speak at the small church-related university where I taught. Alumni and other supporters were loud in their objection to this decision. Already frustrated and threatened by her public attacks on church privileges, they were outraged that she was invading those acres that were supposedly one of the few protected, Christ-dedicated spots left. On the evening of her lecture the greater threat to Christian faith, from my observation, lay in the unlovely hatred displayed by some would-be defenders of the faith. The students, many of whom showed a fine Christian spirit, knew the age in which they were living and entered intelligently into its dialogues.

American Pluralism

Actually, this struggle between pluralism and the idea of a theocratic or monolithic society goes back to the beginnings of the United States. Recently it has simply shifted into a more radical phase in an altered context.

When our forebears created a new nation two hundred years

ago, there was no chance that any one denomination could become the established religion because of the great mixture and diversity within the colonies. Many church people were unhappy about this, but two strong groups favored separation of church and state—free church groups, like the Baptists, and many of the political leaders who were deists urging religious freedom. In the decades since then this "lively experiment" in pluralism has worked well and proved widely popular.

However, from the start of the American nation the vast majority of its people have had some common ideas and ideals. Without an established religion, these ideals have often taken on a transcendent or religious mystique, or power. People could easily base these ideas upon the Bible or the principles of the Protestant Reformation. One scholar has summarized "the American democratic faith" in four broad ideas:

1. The universe contains a framework of fixed principles, both physically and morally.

2. Human beings are free, rational, worthful, and responsible individuals.

3. Belief in progress, all kinds, but especially progress for the individual in building the principles of the universe into one's own character and life.

4. Manifest Destiny for this people and nation, a kind of progress-thinking for the nation.

These ideas were vague, but deeply ingrained. Freedom was one of the best catchwords for representing this whole complex of feelings and convictions. Even more vaguely it was felt that God was behind this kind of universe, to uphold it. Furthermore, the motto was *E Pluribus Unum,* "one composed of many." It was believed that the diversity of pluralism was caught up in the unity of nationhood.

By the time of the Civil War this unity, never very explicit, came to look more and more like a Protestant version of Christendom—an American, free-church Protestantdom. Revivals had become crusades aimed at converting the newly burgeoning cities. One historian writes on nineteenth-century Protestant history under the heading "Righteous Empire," stressing how a variety of campaigns to improve society and its morals tended to interpret national unity as a melting pot that would make everybody into WASPs. This effort to Christianize the society into a Protestant pattern had obviously failed by the turn of the century. This doesn't mean that there are not even today Protestants who fight for "Christian turf" in America, witness the furor a Madalyn Murray O'Hair can stir up. But this mood is essentially a jaundiced hangover.

However, that leaves a large question mark over the meaning of national unity. By the 1920s and 1930s our crusading for freedom and democracy, even our confidence in progress and in Manifest Destiny had wavered badly.

At the same time all the philosophical bases for our four common convictions had disappeared. This is illustrated by what had happened to our idea of a human being. Darwin tied us closely to the animals. Marx stressed the way we are determined by our economic circumstances. Freud showed the power of subconscious forces within us to exercise control. In the mid-twentieth century one had to go against the grain of the thought-world to assert belief in a free, rational, responsible, worthful individual.

Furthermore, in recent decades Americans have become sensitized to the way in which majorities oppress minorities, sometimes blatantly, but frequently subtly and unconsciously. All this recent ethnic consciousness has contributed much to recognition of human particularity and the richness of traditions. But it sharpens still more the question of unity or cohesion in our society. Not only do we not want a melting pot, we can hardly envision a good vegetable soup with any consistency to it!

One more compelling fact rounds out this argument that Americans now live in the vastly changed situation of a truly radical pluralism. That fact is that we live in a global village today. Nineteenth-century Americans had some space in which to work out their unity and their destiny. It makes some sense to consider American Christianity as an evolving movement in itself during that century. But in the late twentieth century both American Christians and American religious life must be viewed from a worldwide perspective.

It is still important to ask what commonality binds together the citizens of this one *commonwealth.* It becomes even more necessary to ask what commonality—commitments, ideas, values—holds together the one humanity that inhabits this shrinking globe in increasing numbers. This chapter is concerned with the role of the church in such a radically pluralistic society.

The Church's Setting

It is from the global perspective that one can most readily discern the end of Christendom. Four phrases can quickly summarize the situation of the church in today's world. The first phrase is "a hostile environment." On the one hand, this is evidenced in an increasing secularism in which people are quite indifferent to traditional religion, also whole areas of life, entire blocks of people, even generations of people, who are cut off from the accents of the religious traditions. And this secularism is worldwide today. On the other hand, there are counterfaiths: some of them ancient religions revived, and others false and biased ideologies that take on the fanaticism of religion. There is even a new popularity for belief in horoscopes and other lingering superstitions. All of these are competitors of Christianity and are mostly hostile to it.

The second phrase to describe the church in our day is "a worldwide fellowship." Though a small minority in most places, Christianity is spread pretty well across the globe. One can no longer say that a certain geographic territory can be identified as Christian. In the United States we have to send missionaries into our great universities and our urban ghettos. And there are real evidences of native and vital Christianity scattered throughout areas of the globe that used to be strange to the accents of the gospel. Christianity is to be found wherever one finds the Holy Spirit at work.

The third phrase to describe the church today is "pruning time." It is a time of sifting, a time of testing for the church. Many nominal Christians have fallen away or been torn away. It is a time of conflict with the culture rather than domestication within it. Much of the dead wood has already been torn away or cut off. Some of the buds and shoots—signs of renewal—are beginning to appear.

This leads to the fourth phrase to describe the church, namely "a period of rediscovery." As the great hedge that was Western culture is pruned severely, one can see the separate bushes of which it consists—including one particular bush called the church, now revealing its individual identity as distinct from both the state and other aspects of the culture. This means an opportunity to rediscover traditions in theology, liturgy, and the church's life. It means, in the ecumenical movement, the rediscovery of the church as unity and mission.

The Church's Shape

What does all this mean for the shape of the church itself in this late twentieth century?

Most conspicuously it means that the church has become a *self-conscious minority,* possessing no territory, and no longer embedded in a particular society. Surrounded by secular or hostile forces, church people know that they are a small minority everywhere in the world. We have become newly aware of ourselves as one type of people among a diversity of quite different people, which forces us to recover our bearings and to rediscover our identity. Two questions loom large.

Suddenly, we need urgently to know in a new light: Who are all these other people with whom we brush shoulders, who crowd our television sets? Since we can no longer push them to the fringes of our consciousness or pigeonhole them carefully within our system, we had better take a new, more sensitive look at them. Who are the Jews? Who are the devotees of Eastern religions? Who are the American Indians? Who are the poorest people in our midst? What are Chinese communists really like? What kind of political systems will Africans want for themselves? American Christians must rapidly get into such questions as these at a deep level—both for their own self-understanding and as part of their Christian service in this age (see chapter 6).

Even more basic for people who have recently become a self-conscious minority, is a second question: Who are we? What does it mean to be a Christian and to be the Christian church within a polyglot global village?

To answer this question Christians are pushed back once more into careful examination of their sources. When a hedge is trimmed so that a particular bush stands exposed, I would presume that the leaves and twigs become newly concerned about their roots.

This means Bible study. It also means a more lively concern for the central traditions of the church (the stem and main branches, if you please) and renewed interest in the power, presence, and inspiration of the Holy Spirit (dare I suggest sap?). But primarily it means serious study of the Bible. Fortunately, among Catholics and Protestants there has been for several decades a resurgence of interest both in biblical scholarship and in grass-roots Bible study for the laity. The church's renewal and its proper response to this age of liberation and pluralism both depend on the surge of this movement.

Among the more than eighty analogies for the church in the

New Testament, one basic image has emerged as the most helpful for Christians in the late twentieth century. It is that of the *People of God.* In the Old Testament, God rescued the Israelites from their slavery in Egypt, led them into the wilderness, and created a free people who agreed to be his priesthood and nation. Drawing on this idea, the author of I Peter puts it succinctly for Christians: "But you are a chosen race, a royal priesthood, a holy nation, God's own people, that you may declare the wonderful deeds of him who called you out of darkness into his marvelous light. Once you were no people but now you are God's people" (2:9-10).

To be equally succinct, in this passage are three great truths about the nature of the church. (1) This is God's doing, making a people out of those who were no people, but were mere slaves or chattel. (2) Those slaves have been called out of darkness and into light, out of slavery and into liberation as God's own people. (3) They are called for a purpose: to be a royal priesthood that declares God's wonderful deeds. Through God's action a people is created and called to declare God's deeds to other people.

If, then, we take these truths defining who we really are and apply them to the circumstances of the church in the modern world, there is a congruence: they fit. In the twentieth century God is once again calling the church out of its too tight involvement with a particular society—Western civilization or Christendom—to be a people set apart, his holy nation. The purpose of this disentanglement is not to withdraw from the world, but to enter the world again in a new way, as God's priesthood of agents witnessing to his marvellous deeds. This dual action is caught up in the familiar phrase "in but not of the world," and provides a rhythm for the motions of the modern church. Christians move back and forth between their sources and their neighbors, and between Bible study and vigorous dialogue with those other modern people newly rediscovered.

The church becomes energy itself, oscillating between opening to God's renewing power and an expenditure of itself in priestly service to God's humankind.

Translated into the life of a congregation, this becomes the rhythm of gathering and scattering, of coming together among ourselves to celebrate and to study, then going forth among all those other people for the bulk of the week, carrying out our ministry among them. This is the pattern of Sunday's retreat and renewal, followed by Monday's new penetration into the weekday world as God's peculiar people.

Paratroopers

Molly Batten has likened a congregation to a company of paratroopers dropped behind enemy lines each Monday morning, with expectation of making their way back to the supply depot on the following Sunday. This is a good image for two reasons. It makes clear the twofold nature of the church's life, namely the back-and-forth rhythm of the people of God. Even more, this image suggests that the gathered congregation's life should be like a supply depot and place of retreat for battle-weary troops. In such a situation there would be an air of intense preparation surrounding all the activities—the worship, the preaching, the education, and the auxiliary programs. The subject matter would be geared to meet the demanding circumstances and decisions awaiting the troops in the weekday ahead. There would be no place any more for the "bleacher Christian." Discipline would be rigorously maintained so that all the troops stay in shape. Functional cells would multiply—focusing upon Bible study, prayer, care of the sick, decision-making, and personal help for each participant. People would gather together with others in the congregation facing similar assignments in the coming week. The congregation would be eager to join in with the planning of the larger regiment and the whole military unit to insure that its paratroopers are not left without support. In many congregations there would be desertions and losses, but as the congregations became smaller there would be higher morale and stronger fellowship.

Of course, a military analogy with reference to enemy lines doesn't accurately reflect the attitudes Christians carry into their weekday associations. We would hope to be more like harbingers of love in our daily contacts. But we do have to become increasingly aware that we are a peculiar people, and that our commitments and convictions are going more and more against the grain of the culture as a whole. Probably the lifestyles we adopt will contrast sharply with those of our neighbors. We cannot expect our children to be shaped by public education and public entertainment into young people with an acceptable set of Christian values.

In other words, even mainline American Christianity will take on more of the contours of a sect than heretofore. A sect is an exclusive religious group, in contrast to a denomination, or more "churchly" religious body. While this exclusiveness may take the various forms of adult-only membership, claiming to be the only true church, or withdrawing from society, still the central definition of a sect—in this context—is that it insists upon a disciplined membership with a comparatively high level of commitment. It is in this sense—disciplined, committed membership—that the demands of the age are calling American Christians into a more sectarian form of church life.

For practical purposes this means raising the standards of active membership. There can continue to be broad lists of nominal members, but it ought to become clear that those who exercise the power of active commitment constitute the core of the magnetic force, whereas all the others are part of the great field upon which that force seeks to work. Even shut-ins can be active in prayer and involved in prayer groups. More and more it becomes imperative to envision the active congregation as a honeycomb of cells—prayer cells, Bible-study cells, personal-support cells, various kinds of social-action cells, evangelism cells, spiritual-healing cells, etc. Those who are not within the honeycomb of cells are not within the covenanted, committed, active membership. Corporate worship will remain central, but its fervor and texture will emerge from the cells that undergird its reality through their action and interaction. Perhaps it would be better to speak of nuclear congregations, rather than to draw the analogy with a sect. In years ahead it will inevitably cost more to be an evident Christian. Some will take up the discipline; others will fall away. A nucleus will carry the thrust of the church into the societies of the future.

Unlike a typical sect, however, the nucleus will always know that it is an integral part of the surrounding world, and that its purpose is sacrificial service to that world. A nucleus is part of a larger whole. A priesthood comes from the people it serves, and knows that it remains essentially a part of that whole people, even as it seeks to relate them to God. We're therefore talking about a disciplined sect that serves, a minority that knows it exists for all those other minorities that together make up the human race.

The image of paratroopers suggests all this. But three familiar biblical images are even more apt—light, salt, and leaven. The sun in the sky, a light bulb, or light through a window are all minority features in their respective landscapes, yet they function powerfully and helpfully, affecting the whole scene. Salt is a tiny ingredient in most foods, but it is essential to the proper flavor of the whole mass of food. It is the little leaven that transforms the whole lump of dough. We used to stress the image of the church as a grain of mustard seed that grows quickly into an impressive bush. For the decades ahead we must shift that image toward the creative minorities of light, salt, and leaven.

One serious warning goes with this scenario. It does not mean abandoning any present strengths, such as votes, political leverage, economic clout, or ecclesiastical authority. All these may desert us as we lose or loosen our hold on the older societies, and they on us. But where we now have these influences, let's exercise them wisely for the sake of humanity. There are many immediate battles—human rights, food for the poor, justice for political prisoners, control of pornography—in which it is worth investing ourselves.

In fact, during this transition period it is probably important to add to the images of the nuclear congregation and the disciplined sect functioning as a creative minority, a third image, that of the bold, beleaguered bishop whom the common people love and support as he fights for the poor and oppressed, in sharp conflict with a military/industrial dictatorship. There are a number of these brave leaders in the world today, and there should be at least a few in the United States in the decades ahead. The best example at present—Dom Helder Camara, Archbishop of Olinda and Recife in Brazil—fits in our story better at a later point (chapter 8).

It would be logical to follow up this impressionistic preview of the church's role in the decades ahead with a more specific description of the kinds of services the church should be offering modern humanity. We shall do this later. But first we must take a closer look at the lay Christian's role in modern society both as a part of the church (chapter 4) and as one who tries to make ethically Christian decisions (chapter 6), together with a look at a promising trend in contemporary theology (chapter 5).

Chapter Four

Where Are the Supply Trains?

A Serious Failure

If the church is people, the People of God, then most of the church spends most of its time beyond religious activities, ecclesiastical organizations, and the direct leadership of the clergy. That is obvious.

Out of a devastated Europe at the end of World War II emerged a movement which stressed that lay people provide the church's ministry in the weekday, "secular" world. The faintness of this lay witness, it was claimed, has been the chief reason of the church's weakness in the turmoils and troubles of the twentieth century. This movement, the Lay Renaissance, issued a call for "the ministry of the laity," a phrase that has been quite popular for fifteen years in America. You will recognize this theme as one major focus for the book you are reading.

But the Lay Renaissance has brought no real change. Little that is new is happening. Renaissance means rebirth, but there is little rebirth. Ministry means service in Christ's name. However, many lay people either don't know how that translates into their daily lives or are not motivated to do it. Furthermore, those who are doing it go unrecognized in church circles. It is the argument of this chapter that *the major problem is the failure to provide resources at the very place of ministry.*

Elliott Couden, with his anguished cry amid the howling winds of that Seattle mountain peak, has felt and voiced the essence of the problem: The supply trains are missing! How can liberators move out without support?

A few hardy lay people do move out into their weekday world with a well-focused ministry. When problems multiply, when conflicts emerge, when decisions are tough, these people often find their church associations chopping them up rather than supporting their attempts at ministry.

My friend Bill Diehl, in his book *Christianity and Real Life,*[1] illustrates this beautifully with incidents from his own life and from the lives of friends and acquaintances. For example, Nancy, a committed Christian with a talent for group work, became increasingly involved in community organizations seeking to provide housing for the poor. This left her with less time for church activities. Criticisms from church friends heightened her sense of guilt about this. But her greatest disappointment came when she took leadership in controversial efforts at prison reform. Church people criticized her for being a troublemaker rather than a peacemaker. She could find encouragement and support under tension only from her secular friends in the community endeavor. She felt totally abandoned by her church when she took seriously her Christian ministry in the community.

Bill Diehl, who continues to be a leader in church circles, sums up his experience like this: "My church," he says, "has always told me that my active life in the congregation's worship and study will send me out to be a 'little Christ' to others whom I meet. It *says* that, but it *does* nothing to support my ministry in the various arenas of my life."

> I am now a sales manager for a major steel company. In the almost thirty years of my professional career, my church has never once suggested that there be any type of accounting of my on-the-job ministry to others. My church has never once offered to

improve those skills which could make me a better minister, nor
has it ever asked if I needed any kind of support in what I was
doing. There has never been an inquiry into the types of ethical
decisions I must face, or whether I seek to communicate the faith to
my co-workers. I have never been in a congregation where there
was any type of public affirmation of a ministry in my career. In
short, I must conclude that my church really doesn't have the least
interest in whether or how I minister in my daily work. . . .

I am not alone in my disillusionment. On the basis of personal
conversations as well as surveys conducted by the churches
themselves it is obvious to me that many other laypeople too feel
that the church has all but abandoned them in their weekday
world.[2]

Diehl's book drew its title from a conversation with a man who
had been a serious Christian for decades. The man quoted
Paul's "Whatever you do, do it for the glory of God," adding
that he supposed Paul was speaking about Christianity. "But,"
this man asserted as his new insight, "I think it can apply in real
life as well."[3] So wide is the gap between Christian experience
and real life.

Our family once had an excellent cleaning lady who was also a
churchgoer. Nadine simply never connected those two parts of
her life—her ability to serve and her Christian faith. After asking
her about her life several times, I wrote up what she was saying:

I *have* to do cleaning and scrubbing. It's been the only way I can
make money to finish raising five kids since my husband's death
ten years ago.

It's hard work too. I don't believe for a minute that a mop can do
the job in scrubbing kitchen and bathroom floors. Mops just
redistribute the dust. I'm not afraid to get down on my knees and
go at it. That seems to be unusual today and I could do two weeks
of work every week, for all the women who want my help.

I get some satisfaction out of it, too. Not that I would choose this
kind of work if I had the education for some other jobs. But my
mother was blind the last eleven years of her life, and I had to stop
school after one year in high school. Don't believe I didn't cry that
fall when my friends went back for their sophomore year.

The good part of my work is that I am often with people I like. To some extent I can choose now which homes I'll clean, really which women I want to work for. I like to be sociable and enjoy the talk and friendliness of some homes and housewives. Not that I just stand around and gab.

And, when you ask me, I can agree that I like to go into a dirty house and make it clean. There's a satisfaction in doing a thorough job of cleaning a floor, a room, a whole house. Week by week I come to feel that this home is my responsibility and that this woman and family need my help. After a while I don't mind either if my job gets held up because of baby sitting (or pet care), telephone answering, bed-making, and things like that. And I feel like part of the family at the lunch table.

I guess an important part of it is that people come to trust me. Maybe at 9 a.m. the wife explains that she must take the children shopping in Baltimore, and at noon her husband rushes in and out on his way to the golf course, leaving me taxi money. All day I work hard so that she'll be pleased with the clean house when she gets back. And I figure I work harder than usual (even though I get paid by the hour) to prove something to myself.

Why do I do that? I suppose you're right that I want to think I'm a person people can trust. Or you could say that I just think people should be that way.

Do I relate these work attitudes to my Christian faith and my church attitudes? The answer is no. I never have thought things through like that. I've been attending Sunday school or church since I was a little girl, belonging to Lutheran churches since I was eight. I can't say I attend real faithfully, but I'm an active member of our Sunday school class and I believe the things that are taught there. Sure, I can agree, after you point it out, that my desire to be good at scrubbing and cleaning and to be trusted in my work probably has a lot to do with my belief in God and his creation and the purposes that God has for human beings. I just never thought much about it in that way.[4]

True, some Christians make good connections across that gap. But who helps them? What advisors can they find? Who supports them? Who accepts their confessions and helps them weigh their alternatives in difficult decisions? No wonder such Christians are in scarce supply!

An explicit and articulate Evangelical Christian steps into the White House to a lonely post with very tough decisions. The magazines are full of descriptions of the many specialists with whom he has surrounded himself. Does Jimmy Carter have people with whom he can discuss the relation between his Christian convictions and his presidential responsibilities? Are there support groups, personal and theological, ready to advise and encourage? If there are, it is almost accidental from the standpoint of the church's knowing what it is about and structuring itself accordingly.

Two centuries ago, at the beginnings of our nation, the distances were not so great. Recently I read a bicentennial biography of John Witherspoon, the powerful preacher brought from Scotland to head Princeton College. I was amazed all over again at the ease with which he combined church leadership with political leadership, helping to carry New Jersey into independence and the federal republic, becoming famous as a signer of the Declaration of Independence, and all without ever getting far from Princeton and his churchly posts.

What has happened during the intervening two centuries? Why is the distance so great, and what has become of the lay movements that, for a while, appeared to bridge the gap? I can use only shorthand phrases and a few symbols to show what has happened in American life.

The Nineteenth Century

In the eighteenth and nineteenth centuries in Western civilization, especially in its Protestant parts, the following trends and movements were ascendant or rising to dominance: rationalism, liberalism, scientific thinking, progress-thinking, the middle class, political democracy, economic laissez-faire, and religious tolerance. For our purposes let me stress four other "isms." Most important is *individualism*. Probably at no other point in history were people so plausibly able to view themselves as *free-standing individuals,* pulled loose from a chain of heredity, no longer embedded in a natural/geographic environment, or defined primarily by an economic position or a social structure such as a clan or nation or church hierarchy.

Right away it becomes obvious that the United States of America was born in that atmosphere and carried that Enlightenment ideology into the late twentieth century. Furthermore, its citizens are still deeply imbued with that understanding of what a human being is.

Our second "ism," more basic and durable enough to last through the twentieth century, is *secularism.* This means, increasingly, that not only is life cut off from any transcendent reference, but also that there are many areas of human endeavor that stay separate from each other. A unifying force is lacking. A university becomes a multiversity.

Our third "ism" is secularism's natural companion, *pluralism,* or thought systems existing side by side with no points of reference, such as ethnic or religious groups which have no commonality except the same space. When John Witherspoon helped this nation come to birth, pluralism had made great progress, but there was considerable commonality of understanding of the universe, its moral structures, and what a human being is. Now that is all washed away. As we noted in chapter 3, the pluralism of today is a radical phenomenon among us.

Meanwhile—and here is our central point in this compact historical essay—in the eighteenth century, individualism and secularism/pluralism combined to produce another social effect, our fourth "ism"—but not an "ism" at all—*atomization.* To atomize means to view or treat as if made up of discrete or atomistic units. People felt like separate units, in that they were not quite so pressured by society. There was more space between the major social institutions of the day. Presumably the independent small farmer had it made. Voluntary association provided enough impetus to fulfill many needs in society. An individual man or woman could more readily "get it all together" within one person's life and understanding.

And, let us hasten to add, the churches of the era fit the spirit of the age. Left-wing, free-church, voluntarist Protestantism, crushed on the continent in the seventeenth century, had struggled into the position of recognized dissenters in eighteenth-century England, and finally came into their own in nineteenth-century America. Just at the time Christendom was beginning to shatter, a freewheeling Protestantdom had a brief heyday in the United States in the mid-1800s.

Seventeenth-century Puritans had not only stressed the sovereignty of God, they also had a vivid sense of the lordship of Christ over all of life, including both political and economic life. At that time the dominant pietism—whether continental Lutheran, Methodist, or revivalist American—started with individual conversion and sent individual volunteers into eager crusades. There were forays into many regions, but not often into economics. They won discrete victories for Christ across the continent and in missionary efforts around the globe.

Here were the great lay movements of the nineteenth and early twentieth centuries, rooted in local congregations but becoming national in scope. An army of lay people carried them: the Sunday school movement, the YMCA and YWCA, the temperance movement, a great variety of missionary and Bible societies, the Student Christian Movement, the Student Volunteer Movement, the Red Cross, all kinds of reform efforts and welfare programs. There was magnificent lay leadership and energy—a great Christian outpouring, through which the church flowed outside its ecclesiastical structures. The Christian movement in the United States has been called an experiment in Christianity with a minimum of church. It certainly fit the age: individualistic, atomistic, pluralistic, voluntary associations doing battle with secular forces in an optimistic atmosphere.

The Twentieth Century

The twentieth century is a drastically different age. It is the *Collective Age*. Secularism has moved more deeply into the fabric of our society. The pluralism is much more radical. The free space is gone. Atomization has disappeared. The free-standing individual is an unlikely critter. Individualism as an idea doesn't fit this age at all, except in the form of selfish rip-off.

Nor is there any longer a clear connection in our society between the common life and the Christian tradition, or the activities of the worshiping clique. Public worship isn't public. In the center city you have to look far down the canyons between the great buildings to find any church spires. In the typical suburb the tower of the community church is lost in the forest of TV aerials.

In fact, there isn't much that remains of any *common life* or *community*. We live in one tight little world, geographically and technologically speaking, in which people with widely divergent ideas and experiences jostle each other. Radically one world, radically pluralistic. Modern humanity is thrust into synthetic and uneasy togetherness, with many worlds intersecting, many values criss-crossing, many ideologies competing, and many people mixing with each other. As our means of communicating multiply, our thought worlds divide and clash. As we approach the power of instant, worldwide media coverage of an event or experience, we find it increasingly hard to say anything that will be true for all listeners or to do anything that will be understood by all observers. Not only does the church no longer provide the uniting focus, but nothing else has taken its place. There is no common focus.

For our purpose the best and most vivid image is that of *pyramids of power*. There are massive social structures into which people must fit, and most individuals fit into more than one. These pyramids are complex and complexly interrelated.

Each becomes not only an arena for social coercion but also provides an ideology, as well as an ethos. Each tries to become a way of life for its inhabitants. The skyscrapers stand cheek by jowl and the narrow streets between them are congested. Our lives are frequently split between them, but often our real life is embedded in one of them. We really belong to the oil industry, the medical profession, the summer-home-by-the-lake recreators, the university structures, a political party, or you name it. Some of us really belong in that ancient wobbly edifice of waning power called the family, where we make our little nests among the available rooms.

Good communication takes place only horizontally between those on the same level of the pyramid or hierarchy of power, whether within one pyramid or across the canyon, from the thirty-fourth floor of one pyramid to the thirty-fourth floor of another. Therefore, the way to power and influence is by rising to the top of your particular heap. Then, and relatively easily, you can communicate with and influence those at the other peaks.

The View from the Religion Tower

Now the clergy, as professionals, live primarily in the religion pyramid, within the ecclesiastical structures. Church structures have sometimes been described as the ghetto where the clergy dwell, and sometimes as a bewildering number of variegated buildings that house the many denominations. But here we are thinking of the church as together constituting one impressive skyscraper.

If the clergy want influence, they move up that pyramid. If they want to influence other pyramids, they support the bishops on the eightieth floor as the bishops communicate with the generals, the governors and representatives, the corporation heads, the Hollywood celebrities, and all top-of-the-heap people on the eightieth floors of other pyramids.

Aside from a few domesticated or clericalized laity, the bulk of lay people are amateurs. They do not live primarily in the religion pyramid, and they do not generally move up in its structures. A few will get high up in some other pyramid and thus be invited onto the top floors of the religion building. Jimmy Carter can now do that any time, if he has any time! Most lay people, though, come into the ground floor as amateurs, as clients. Like clients anywhere else, they count for little as individuals. They could organize to lobby, like Nader's Raiders or Common Cause, but they'll soon hire professionals if they want to be successful, and their new structure will soon be its own tower affixed to the remainder of our towering religious pyramid.

Great lay movements *are* no more. Those of a century ago have been absorbed into ecclesiastical structures—Sunday schools, Student Christian movements, missionary and Bible societies, tract and publishing societies, and numerous welfare institutions. In place of some, the government has taken over, or they've become pyramids of their own—the Ys, the Red Cross, and the private colleges. While there are some interesting religious movements involving lay people—the charismatics, for example—there are no important forays into the public domain. Our social structures no longer permit it. Most lay people have settled for a meek client relationship, receiving services from their religious specialists, the clergy.

Generally speaking, they get pretty good service, probably better than ever before. Many clergy touch the personal and religious lives of many lay persons for significant good. I am certainly not advocating doing away with the professional clergy, or undoing those careful systems for their education. Nor do I advocate doing away with the religion pyramid, for it would be folly even to try. Such destruction wouldn't accomplish anything. Nor am I simply a nostalgic who's longing for great lay movements once more.

Where Are the People?

What is truly disturbing—if the church *is* people, the People of God—is that 90 plus percent of them are only casually, (mainly as clients) in and out of the religion pyramid and under clergy leadership. We speak of clergy as leaders of the church. Yet a high percentage of that church spends most of its time scattered throughout all those other pyramids. So, whatever your doctrine of the hidden or invisible church may be, most of the church remains invisible to its leaders, except when they focus binoculars on the windows of those other buildings, or enter other first floors as clients themselves, or receive that occasional invitation to visit a few floors up.

When I was a mission pastor, there was a Mrs. Blix. She was very active in our services and programs at first. Thereafter she remained a regular attender, but disappointed me by drawing back as a congregational leader. The reason, as I understood it, was because neither she nor I could get her son or husband to take an interest in the church. Three years later one of my good members mentioned that it was because of Mrs Blix that she had begun to attend our congregation. That rang a bell; I had heard that before. I checked my records and was astounded to see that, in our small group, twenty people had mentioned Mrs. Blix as an instrumental force in their entry into our church life. Suddenly, I accidentally discovered that she was doing something right "out there." She was really witnessing. When I spoke to her about this it became obvious that she was unaware of any success in witnessing, because her husband and son still didn't come to church. By the power of the Holy Spirit she was exerting real Christian leadership, but neither she nor I nor anyone else had any grasp of it. And there I was, the religious leader for that group, accidentally discovering a little bit of the results!

Let me use another example of my own obtuseness, an example which will also further our argument. For a decade before 1965, I had been caught up in the Lay Renaissance. While it was not a lay movement, by any means, I did meet or learn about some lay people who were articulate witnesses in their daily work, folks like the realtor Elliott Couden. I began the volume *My Job and My Faith,* in which a number of these people would tell their story by answering these four questions:

1. What is your job and what does it mean to you?

2. What are the kinds of routine decisions your job requires you to make?

3. What do you consider to be the Christian dimensions of those decisions?

4. What do you consider to be the major resources available to you as you make the decisions your job requires?

When their chapters came to me, one by one, I looked them over as a seminary professor and decided that, with exceptions, the theology in them was scanty and shallow. But I reread them more thoughtfully and changed my mind. I found more of the phrases of traditional theology than I'd seen at first glance. More significantly, remembering the assignment I had given them, I realized that I had received from each person a working philosophy of life, a rationale for his or her various commitments, and a description of a style of life and a ministry. In other words, what they had given me was a genuinely functional set of theologies to support their daily ministries. Yet, even though I had asked for it, I had trouble finding it.

It is with such material that the professional theologian should start to work. But it is very hard for a trained theologian to see it, even when it has been dug out for that person—partly because it seems to have so little to do with the patterns of formal theology.

Forty-five years ago a famous lay Christian, John R. Mott, in his book, *Liberating the Lay Forces of Christianity,* described with some plausibility how lay persons can help to educate the young, to finance the operation of the congregation, to touch people of influence, and, in one long paragraph without any break from the rest of the list, to proclaim the gospel in society. Listen to how he put it:

> Laymen are needed on every hand and in all relationships of everyday life to proclaim the full Gospel—individual and social—and to demonstrate its power. Society today is so complex, life is so fully organized (in fact overorganized), and human activity is so highly specialized or departmentalized, that the only way adequately to permeate and influence it all for Christ and the Church is through laymen who, within the sphere of their daily calling and relationships, actually show forth Christ. Have we a religion which can locate and remove causes of industrial and racial misunderstanding, ill will, and strife, as well as deal with their serious results? What message has the Christian Church for the hungry and embittered unemployed? What program have we who are members for doing away with darkened, overcrowded, unhealthful tenements? Have we dynamic truth from God which should stir conscience to action because of injustices, cruelties, and abominations which are still permitted within the range of the influence of the Christian Church? The clergy may answer these penetrating questions aright, but they alone cannot give the answers full effect.[5]

In 1931 Mott assumed the clergy were the real leaders. "I do not share the view that the Christian ministry does not have so important and so necessary a function as in the past. As much as ever the clergy is called upon to lead, and, to this end, to build up, to train, to inspire, and to *direct* the lay forces." Thus, Mott could approvingly quote Lyman Beecher, who, asked why his ministry at a prominent church was so successful, said, "I preach on Sunday, but I have 450 men and women who go out every day in the week to translate into life and service the message which I have sought to lodge in their hearts."[6] That picture still persists, even while the lay ministry disappears before the clergyperson's eyes.

No wonder many of the clergy have been confused about their role in recent decades. What may have been possible a century ago is not possible today. Clergy cannot provide all the leadership and direction for lay ministry in the world. Several decades ago a theologian noted the "maceration" of the minister. Maceration means "wasting away," and it aptly described what the clergy was experiencing.

What is needed is the realization that both clergy and laity have leadership roles, but they are different roles. The clergy are primarily responsible for the assembled phase of the church's life. They are called and trained as professionals to preach, lead worship, educate in the tradition, provide religious or theological counsel, and lead the congregation's organizational and fellowship life. Lay leadership in those areas is important, but supportive and secondary. On the other hand, that whole assembled phase of the church's life, though it has its own integrity, should undergird and support lay ministry during the scattered phase of the church's life. Members of the clergy should be quite aware that one of their basic tasks is helping to equip the laity for their weekday ministry. Neither the assembled nor the scattered phase is more important, but the church (i.e., the People of God) spends much more time in the latter phase. Similarly, neither clergy nor laity is more important, but many more of the church are laity.

If this duality is not kept clearly in mind, there will continue to be a maceration of the ministry of the clergy. More pertinent for this book, there will also continue to be a laceration of the laity in their attempts at ministry.

Furthermore, clergy within the religion pyramid cannot package resources for lay people to carry out and use in their various pyramids. The Word of God cannot be encapsuled at the worship service so that it can be carted away, opened, and applied somewhere "out there."

Imagine that your life situation is a cubicle on the eighth floor of the lawyers' pyramid. You look around and say, "Hey, I've got to bring something in to change this setting, if I'm really trying

51

to represent the church's life here.'' So you go down and over to the religion pyramid. Back you come with a package given you by a clergyperson. You open it at your desk. What will it be? Maybe it's a handful of seeds, because the Bible speaks of the Word of God as seed. What will you do with that in your cubicle in your pyramid? Or maybe it is dynamite for a few bombs, since the Bible refers to the explosive power of the gospel. What will you do with that? Such mixed metaphors seem an appropriate way to stress how hard to handle most sermons are, even most biblical images, when applied directly to the complexities of modern life. Clergy can assist, but lay people will have to make their own difficult translations for their own decisional lives.

Seeds and Shoots

Let's turn from critical analysis to more constructive ideas and suggestions for the remainder of the chapter. Let's retain our image of the pyramids that divide up modern life so threateningly. Let's remind ourselves of the image of the church as paratroopers dropped every Monday behind enemy lines (chapter 3). Does the picture of parachutes among the pyramids suggest a Christian posture for modern life? Under this image dynamite could indeed be an appropriate resource for the Christian's daily tasks. But let's also take seriously the biblical image of seed.

One veteran of the Lay Renaissance, John Casteel, has made an assertion that ought to receive serious consideration from all who are concerned about the church's ministry in the modern world. The layperson's situation, he declared, is not simply "a field for the ministry of the Church," but is "the ground within which the Church's own life, understanding, and faith is to be sown and raised up."[7]

Think about that. Sowing seed and cultivating a crop are familiar images. But if the layperson's situation is the soil and the church's own life is the product, then it is not radical enough to talk of translating, as we have done. From seeds to shoots to grain is a sequence of transformation. The gospel and the tradition will be transformed in this process. In fact the human and appropriate Christian correlate for something "to be sown and raised up" is death and resurrection. Now we're talking about a drastic process—death—and about devastating consequences, a radical price to pay. Then, God willing, a startling event transforms the very face of the church, providing the people of God with a new appearance.

If the totality of the church's life is to be discovered anew within every human situation, it will mean for the present leadership of the churches a sowing of seed that will be a dying in Christ, while trusting that God will bring the resurrection. That resurrection will give a foretaste of God's own full harvest, surely marvellous to behold, just as the sight of a few green and tender sprouts can give courage and warmth on a cold day in early Spring.

What does all this mean for the life of a congregation, whether we're talking about seed that has become harvested grain returned to the barn, or whether we're talking about paratroopers who use up their weekly dynamite and return on Sunday to the supply depot?

We've already indicated that for returned paratroopers there should be an atmosphere of preparation, of sharing one's experiences, and of disciplined strategy-making. We've suggested that functional cells would multiply in the areas of Bible study, prayer, care of the sick or disheartened, and personal support through advice, counsel, and encouragement.

All this may not mean great change in the kinds of things congregations do. But it certainly would provide a different perspective, resulting in a greater awareness that these activities are basically an exchange of gifts and burdens. All the People of God would bring from their many situations reports of victories or defeats, discussions of strategies, and an excited sharing of discovered resources. In other words, there'd be an intense give-and-take from out of the diverse situations of lay people, the ground within which the church's own life, understanding, and faith is to be sown and raised up. If only our lay people—encouraged by the clergy—would bring their armfuls of grain and thistles and weeds to the sharing place, the supply depot. Or, to use our third metaphor, if only lay Christians scattered throughout the various pyramids of the metropolis would realize that their journeys to the religion pyramid are not primarily client visits for religious services. Rather, these movements are part of a vast underground network of communication and exchange in which people take in reports from their cubicle, get a hot lunch, and leave with other surveys and reports and a few interesting packages. If that were really the way we viewed congregational life, it would go a long way toward providing those missing supply trains.

A few congregations are making good beginnings in this direction. A congregation in Baltimore recently undertook a special August-September emphasis on lay ministry. There were three dialogue sermons in which members of the congregation dealt with the ministry of listening (done by a school guidance counselor), the ministry of speaking (an advertising executive), and the ministry of caring (a homemaker). The parish newsletter carried several written statements by other lay members describing their ministries. On "Lay Ministry Sunday" there was an order of affirmation for all lay people, and also a special litany of gratitude. Those who attended the service were invited to make their own commitment to ministry by placing a written statement on the offering plate.

In a number of congregations, people are invited to wear their work clothes to the Sunday service nearest Labor Day. At that time daily work as a Christian calling receives special emphasis. One congregation in suburban Chicago has a pre-liturgy period each Sunday morning during which the members discuss with each other those issues or concerns that are important in their lives at that time. Sometimes, when two or more members find themselves engaged in a weekday ministry that has grown out of the congregation's social action thrusts, their roles will be acknowledged as part of the common ministry of that parish. A young woman on the staff of a Florida congregation has the assignment of enabling lay people to identify and carry out their special ministries in life. A number of congregations are now including in their adult education courses in which lay members share skills—such as counseling or first aid or financial advice or letter writing—as a way of multiplying effective lay ministries. Several congregations have found ways—in newsletters or an annual worship event—to hold up and honor the many volunteer services in the public community which are carried out by members of the congregation, paralleling those traditional opportunities for recognition of workers within congregational life. Since lay overseas missionaries are frequently commissioned, some groups are now working out ways to recognize and support lay people who accept essentially missionary duties (whether through church agency or apart from it) in a particularly tough situation in the home community.

In some instances these initiatives are being encouraged by church officials at the state or national level. One California judicatory has a Commission on Lay Ministries with a threefold assignment: developing and sharing models for lay ministry in the secular world, opening up lay volunteer opportunities for service within the institutional church, and doing the same opening up of opportunities beyond the institutional church. A group of New England churches declared a certain day as Volunteer Recognition Sunday to encourage and support volunteer services in the general community. The same thing has happened more recently in Maryland.

In eastern Pennsylvania lay leaders of one church body have

organized themselves to sponsor retreats several times a year, and monthly breakfasts in major cities encouraging business people to face together their work life as an opportunity for Christian decision and service. Perhaps these are straws in a wind that is gaining force. They are just a sampling.

Those Other Pyramids

All that is helpful, but it does not go far enough. What is really needed, beyond anything yet seen, is a system of supply trains—support *out there within those other pyramids.* How can I say what that would look like? After all, I'm a clergyman working in seminaries. And surely support systems would look quite different at different places, in widely varying contexts.

I can, though, suggest that such supply trains would involve at least these three forms. Absolutely crucial would be small support groups of Christians within the same, or at least a similar, place where decisions are made, and where daily routines are lived out. You'll realize that my reference to physical space, a pyramid or a place, is figurative; I'm talking about interrelationships, people linked together for responsible decision-making. That's the setting in which the church needs desperately to discover itself as an active fellowship, *with structures.* Mostly these structures would be informal cell groups made up of people within a certain echelon of authority within a particular spot in society. There would be a sharing of the concerns natural to Christian people at that spot, supporting each other by bringing Christian insights to bear upon the decisions and attitudes taking shape in that specific habitat.

But the structures would go beyond small groups. On a second level there would be, both within particular cities and nationwide, associations of professionals: lawyers, doctors, nurses, social workers, realtors, architects, and others concerned about the ethics of their professions, their interrelationships with other professions, and public responsibilities from the perspective of Christian commitment. Nor would this second order of extra-ecclesiastical structures be limited to professionals. There could be many of these associations—with their meetings and publications—within all major aspects of human existence from the military to the arts, from the oil industry to the recreation manufacturers, from a political party to a particular governmental bureaucracy.

Then, in the third place, there would have to be a large and diverse network of communication, tying into a loose, broad association all those who are eager to carry out an informed and effective lay ministry in their weekday worlds.

Cells and networks like that would constitute a great, new lay movement for the late twentieth century in America. Some of its leaders would be among the great liberators of our day, the change agents who step boldly ahead into the patterns of the future. Other of its leaders, and most of its rank and file, would be engaged in maintaining links, providing supplies and supply trains, and sustaining each other and their neighbors while maintaining a quiet Christian witness in society. A lay movement like that would be a significant groundswell liberation movement for our time.

It would also be a tiny minority within our present church and our society. In fact, I do not even know whether there are people to take up this vision, these structures, and this ministry. Nor do I know how we clergypersons would relate to all these structures, these groups, these meetings. Some clergy would resist such goings-on. Others would probably be effectively helpful by bringing theological resources and, perhaps, Word and sacraments into these structures. Actually, few clergy or laity yet know how preached Word and celebrated sacraments become lived Word and sacrament in secular settings. Too long have we lived in heretical church structures which concretize the Christian life and give corporate identity to the People of God only in the gathered phase of their existence. At any rate, it would be important that the communication network be tied in with the specialists in the religion pyramid without being dominated or managed from that pyramid.

One thing is clear, the initiative must be taken by lay people. If the clergy leads, most laity become passive. Besides, the clergy generally do not know what to look for. They have worked so exclusively with seeds in barn bins and in the sowing process that they instinctively look for seed when they should be finding green shoots. For several decades some of the best lay people have been forming house churches, populating lay retreat centers, and supporting lay associations like Yokefellows in an effort to discover and cultivate their own ministries.[8] The structural penetration that I am advocating here would be much more likely to emerge from such people and such programs than from clergy-directed institutes or from chaplaincies or from denominational programs. Within ecumenical circles—the World Council of Churches—there has recently come a clear call for laity to take up their own shaping for ministry, including Christian fellowships that are outside present ecclesiastical structures.

For more than a decade, under inspiration from Germany's Evangelical Academies, the Lutheran Church in America has supported Faith and Life Institutes, conferences which pick up a public or professional issue—health care, juvenile justice, farmers and world hunger—and develop their programming and participation through lay leaders in those public issues or from professional groups in those fields. Increasingly, Faith and Life Institutes are now emerging at the request or insistence of lay people trying to bring focused Christian insight to bear *within* their own secular structures. Let me also mention two of the many local manifestations of structured (or sustained) Christian groupings within secular settings—Crossings, Inc., in St. Louis, where workshops feature in-depth probing of the work life of

Christian lay people, and also the Cincinnati Experiment, which is organized so business people can meet regularly in small groups to share the problems faced in their jobs, and ask how their faith relates to their work world. There are also instructive instances in which colleges—often with some church constituency and flavor—involve business people or other secular groupings in conferences that start with a serious look at a secular or professional issue and then provide theological perspectives and opportunities for group discussion.

These examples could be the beginnings of structures "out there" for the church. They are parachurches, organizations that parallel the traditional forms of the church's religious life. There are not nearly enough of them, and few of them really penetrate far into our society (or get high up into secular pyramids). Our problem is that most of our church people do not see these happenings as preludes to the future, or ways into a fruitful recovery of the wholeness of church life. Such events ought to be seen as signs of Christians getting into the action of our age.

Of course, such parachurches would primarily be for churchgoers who are loyal to a parish and a denomination. That's where most lay persons are and that's where they should be. Ties to the tradition and the parish are essential. Yet the structuring of lay ministry beyond parish and tradition is equally essential to the life of God's people. How to get the two together? How to provide supply trains?

A movement among Lutherans called Laos in Ministry is a hopeful experiment in holding the two together. Initiated by a handful of aggressive lay leaders, it consistently aims at cultivating lay ministry in the weekday world. Its quarterly newsletter is called "Monday's Ministers." Its conferences, its creeds, commitments, and calls to action thrust toward the careful formation of lifestyles and ministries within the secular pyramids. Laos in Ministry receives denominational endorsement and modest financial support. Its membership has grown in just two years to include good numbers of the "ordinary churchgoers" who are also seeking ways to more effective ministry and service. Their seven-point discipline includes the usual elements of prayer, Bible study, corporate worship, proportional giving, and retreat attendance for personal growth, plus these two:

> The Discipline of Service—To identify one or more specific ministries in life and to allocate sufficient time to carry them out.

> The Discipline of Love—To build a supportive relationship with one or more others with whom I come in daily contact.[9]

Reversing the Trains

Before turning to more specifics about the church's life in the weekday world, we need a last look at the question of supply trains. We've thought about fresh supplies for paratroopers, helpful packages for skyscraper-dwellers, and seed for the farmer's soil. The supply trains, in our image, moved out from the church's assembled life into its scattered existence. For the moment, let's reverse the image: bringing supplies back into the barn.

Does not this year's seed come from last year's harvest, in the natural ordering of things? But suppose we hardly know where that harvest takes place? And what if the supply trains are missing—no wagons or even cultivators, weeders, and threshers? Then where did we get this year's seed? It must be left over from harvests long ago. Isn't it apt to be kind of old, tough, mildewed, or diseased? A feeble Word and stale sacraments? Remember our assertion: "The lay person's situation is not simply a field for the ministry of the church, but is the ground within which the church's own life, understanding, and faith is to be sown and raised up." If the supply trains are missing, we should wonder whether seed from that harvest is getting back into the bins, especially the bin from which next year's planting is to be drawn.

To illustrate the problem let me use our efforts to *understand* the faith, our attempts at *coherence;* in other words, our theology. Who creates our theology? In what ground does it root? Of course it comes from the life of the church, but in what settings, and addressing which questions?

In a quick historical survey, Charles Davis says there have been four major theological "cultures" in church history.[10] Each has had its dominant period, and continues in church life even today. One is *episcopal* theology, written mainly by bishops and expressing the church's episcopal, or overseeing, concern. A second is *monastic* theology, resulting from contemplation and the mystical life. A third is *scholastic* theology, growing out of the university setting. A fourth, dominant today, is the *seminary* theology that has been shaped for the training of a professional clergy. It is not the theology of the bishop, the monk, or the professor, rather it's the theology of the pastor—the congregational leader. This is certainly a valid source for the doing of theology—as are the other three—but if seminaries are too exclusively the seedbed of our theological culture, then we experience what Davis uses as the title of his article: "theology in seminary confinement."

I believe Davis is thus far correct in saying that our professional theologians do not draw effectively on lay experience, lay thinking, and concrete lay lifestyles for their theological work. Therefore I join J. A. T. Robinson in *The New Reformation?* in calling for the cultivation of a new style, a fifth historical type of theological culture, a *genuine lay theology.*

This new approach would have nothing to do with popularizing theology by watering it down for lay consumption. Nor am I talking about lay people attempting formal theology, though lay expressions of their convictions and experiences should be the raw material for a genuine lay theology. I am talking about the professional theologizing that emerges out of the needs and experiences of lay people, that is, attempts to speak to the questions lay people are asking. Robinson calls it "a theology which is impelled by the needs of the *laos,* or whole people of God, to *be* the Church *in* the world."[11] But the supply trains are missing. We have not been listening well, nor have we been receptive to that kind of input.

One modern theological trend which tries to do this receptive listening to lay people is liberation theology. In the next chapter I shall describe this theology, relate it briefly to traditional theology, and show some of its power for the concerns of this volume.

Theology is just one illustration. For its vitality, each aspect of the gathered life of God's people has got to relate to the experiences of those who make up that gathered community, whether they be experiences of piety and God's presence, experiences of human life and the human condition, or experiences of service and Christian ministry.

Chapter Five

Liberation Theology: New and Old

This book reflects two contemporary theological currents. The first is an understanding of the church which stresses that it is the People of God. That idea, recovered from the Bible, has influenced much of the Christian thinking for more than two decades. One expression of it is renewed interest in the weekday ministry of the laity. The second current is liberation theology. Also recovered from the Bible, it is beginning to play a major role in American theological circles in the 1970s. This present volume seeks to bring the insights of liberation theology to focus upon, and to give focus to, the ministry of the laity in the weekday world.

In this chapter let's look more directly at the current liberation theology, then compare it to the Reformation theology that is still authoritative for much American church life, concluding with a discussion of the relation between formal theology and the lay Christian's thinking.

The South American Context

There are numerous liberation theologies. This is not surprising since, as we've discovered, liberation is a broad theme. In the United States, the two more articulate and recognized liberation theologies are those of blacks and women. These are important expressions, both as examples of this theology as formed in the United States and as illustrations of the way Christians who experience oppression think about their experience and their God.

However, on a worldwide scale the most sustained thrust of liberation theology has come from South America. Beginnings of liberation theologies in Africa and the Far East will no doubt blossom in the years ahead. Let me now characterize this theology as it comes from Latin America.

For centuries South America has been the most Christianized part of the present Third World. Since Spanish and Portuguese invaders conquered the Indians in the sixteenth and seventeenth centuries, the Roman Catholic Church has been the established religion for most of the continent through most of the years. By and large it has not raised up a vibrant and native church life. Largely it has supported the rich and the powerful, emphasizing subservience as the chief virtue in both ecclesiastical and public life. For the poor classes and the ordinary people, the Catholic Church until recently has been a part of an oppressive establishment.

In the nineteenth century, Protestant missionaries from the north made some converts. The new Protestant enclaves were people who not only changed their religious views (often coming to a powerful experience of Jesus Christ for the first time) but also changed their lifestyles and entered a kind of counterculture. In that sense Protestantism provided an alternative that offered a measure of liberation from a massive and rigid structure of society and religion. However, by the middle of this century Protestants had become a part of the society in the middle or upper classes. Only the pentecostals and such non-Christian faiths as spiritism presently represent an alternate (largely escapist) pattern of belief and behavior.

Meanwhile, the harsh militaristic colonialism of Spain and Portugal was replaced by the colonialism and economic dominance of Great Britain and then the United States, building up small elites among the ruling classes of the South American nations. Hopes for steady economic development faded by the late 1960s when it became clear that, even in that decade of development, the rich got richer and the poor got poorer. Population growth was rapid, but two-thirds of the people did not have enough to eat, and 20 percent of the people controlled 80 percent of the resources of the continent. Harsh exploitation was built into life for most South Americans.

With the coming of the revolution of rising expectations in the mid-twentieth century, large numbers of Latin Americans became dissatisfied with their mean estate—poverty, ignorance, and powerlessness—and started a conscious search for improvement. Some of them found resources in Marxist patterns of thought for their moves toward greater human fulfillment.

This is a brief, oversimplified background statement against which to set the impact of Vatican II upon the Christians of that continent. In 1968 the Catholic bishops of South America, meeting at Medellin, Columbia, adapted the pronouncements of Vatican II to their continent. They asserted that the Roman Catholic Church belonged on the side of liberation and social justice for South America. Since Latin America, they declared, is obviously in a state of rapid transformation,

> we are on the threshold of a new epoch in the history of our continent. It appears to be a time full of zeal for full emancipation, of liberation from every form of servitude, of personal maturity and of collective integration. In these signs we perceive the first indications of the painful birth of a new civilization.[1]

Since then a number of the bishops have backed away from such exuberance. In the face of the hostility of the increasing number of repressive, right-wing, military governments on that continent, the Catholic Church is now divided. From leaders to rank and file, only a minority are openly committed to social justice concerns. But that still represents a quite significant shift in the role of Catholicism in that part of the world. And it has spawned a vibrant liberation theology. Among the tiny minority of Latin Americans who are Protestant, there are also a few articulate liberation theologians.

The Action/Reflection Method

What is liberation theology? It is first of all a methodology, a way of going about the work of theology. These priests and theologians[2] took a hard look at the people whom they sought to serve. They saw what anyone sees: a poverty-stricken, exploited, overpopulated, and underdeveloped continent, politically unsettled and unable to move out of a deprived, dependent condition. In response to what they saw they did two things. They became social activists, on the one hand, identifying with the poor and oppressed and joining those who worked for change and social justice. On the other hand, they became reflective, analyzing carefully the complex social scene and relating this knowledge to the Bible and their deepest theological insights. This action/reflection method is basic to liberation theology. Out of the combination of action and thought, out of their interplay, comes a worthwhile theology.

An action/reflection method is true to the biblical understanding, these church leaders claim. "God's Word is not understood in the Old Testament as a conceptual communication but as a creative event, a history-making pronouncement. . . . Faith is always a concrete obedience which relies on God's promise." This background "may explain Jesus' use of the word *way* to refer to himself" and why in Pauline literature faith appears as "walking." Then too, in the Johannine literature of the New Testament there is an emphasis upon "*doing* the truth," so that the one who *does* the Word will know the doctrine. There is no room for a purely intellectual grasp of Christian teaching.[3]

Liberation theology is a contextual theology as well, asserting that one's involvement in a particular situation, not only is essential to doing theology, but also inevitably shapes one's Christian experience and the way one makes that experience articulate and coherent (i.e., theology). This contextual emphasis determined the title of one of the clearest expositions of liberation theology in English, called *Doing Theology in a Revolutionary Situation.*

The Bible and the Poor

Out of such experiences and their struggles for justice these theologians/activists immediately found new insights in their reading and grasp of the Bible. This is the second major facet of liberation theology—a particular interpretation of Scripture. They discovered that the gospel is a message for the liberation of oppressed people, and that the Bible is written by oppressed people, out of the experiences of oppressed people. In other words, the Bible speaks more naturally and directly to "the wretched of the earth" than to other people. Like the Argentine priest introduced earlier, these theologians found a key to the Bible (and to the whole human situation vis-à-vis God) in the Exodus and in Jesus' commission from Isaiah in Luke 4:16-30. At many places in Scripture they rediscovered that God has a strong bias toward the poor and the outcast (for example, Jeremiah 22:13-16, Matthew 11:5, 25:31-40, Luke 1:46-55, 16:19-31).

It is not as though poverty is itself a blessed condition. Rather, the Bible speaks of poverty and oppression as degrading and dehumanizing—a scandalous condition in which to hold God's creatures. True, there is a blessed estate called "spiritual poverty"—meaning an openness to God—with which physical poverty may be associated, in contrast to the tendency of the rich to hold onto their own security and possessions. But the main reason for the bias toward the poor is that God wants justice. God's coming kingdom will rectify injustices and provide a fulfilling human existence for all people. Some of these theologians, and the South American Christians who live these ideas, have voluntarily taken up poverty (not a new step among Catholics) to show solidarity with the earth's poor, and to protest the unjust social patterns that perpetuate dire poverty.

History and Justice

The third emphasis of liberation theology follows from the first two. The God known in Christ Jesus and the Bible is the God active in the whole flow of human history, participating in and desirous of shaping all human affairs, including political and economic life. The God who brought the Israelites out of Egypt and, after long struggles in the wilderness, transformed them from slaves to a free nation is the God who today is actively leading his people toward liberation and a just politico-economic system that would in rough fashion anticipate the coming kingdom. Christians cannot, therefore, insist that their God is known only in the special (sacred) history and events surrounding the church's life. Nor can they claim that God functions significantly only in some special inner or spiritual kingdom while the events of nations and economic systems are of minor concern to him. God reigns, and Jesus declares his lordship over the whole human being and the whole enterprise of human society.

Furthermore, these theologians declare, it is a scandal that the inherited theology of the churches has so consistently ignored God's advocacy of the poor and the way in which the huge gap between rich and poor—the power imbalance between the haves and the have-nots—is such a predominating force in the lives of so many human beings. That makes past theologies suspect—written as such theologies have been by the educated and, usually, the economically comfortable.

To help in their analysis of their society and its economic dependence, these men have used some of the ideas of Marxists. They are not Marxists in ideology, and they're certainly not atheists. But they have found in Marxist analysis of society and the struggles between economic classes a useful tool with which to gain perspective on their own situations, as well as a little distance or objectivity in viewing the traditions of Western civilization which had formed them and now served them poorly in their liberation efforts.

I learned this personally through a friend, an Argentine named Mario, who was a leader among Christian students in Uruguay. Trained in theology in a Lutheran seminary and with a doctorate from France, Mario spent several months at the seminary in Ohio where I taught. I learned to know his thinking (and it was passionate thinking) quite well. His ideas could be summarized like this. He believes that Christianity in the Western nations has allowed itself to be used as an ideology that provides a cloak of respectability for an otherwise naked and ugly capitalism. He also is convinced that capitalism inevitably leads to imperialism (specifically, the United States and American corporations in South America). For Mario, imperialism means exploitation of underdeveloped nations, so that these nations remain dependent and poor, with the great majority of their people reduced virtually to slave labor. Meanwhile, he argued, American Christians, when they try to stress "spiritual" answers to all problems and urge individuals to work hard to improve their condition in life, misuse their faith while they personally enjoy affluence at the expense of millions of Latin Americans.

Paulo Freire

All this gives us just a touch of the rich and richly varied theology of liberation coming from the continent to the south during the past decade. It has been powerfully inspiring for many people. Even today, when repressive governments are so brutal and powerful that Latin people are forced to shift the biblical parallel for their daily experience from the Exodus to the Captivity in Babylon, this way of thinking permeates the Christian consciousness of increasing numbers of people.

For church people in the United States—other than several clearly disadvantaged minorities—it is harder to assimilate a theology of liberation, and harder still to identify with either the Exodus or the Babylonian Captivity. We shall have to reexamine our theological assumptions (the subject of a later section). There are other challenging implications for other areas of our lives. Let's look briefly at one area in which there has been direct importation from South America—education.

Paulo Freire of Brazil has become an established figure in adult education programs, his ideas much discussed and used at many place in the world. In his *Pedagogy of the Oppressed* he presents a well-thought-out approach to education. But his main idea can be expressed in terms of his early experiences in literacy programs in Brazil and Chile. In the name of Christ he was working—with words as tools—to free people from a walled-in mind and the subservience that goes with it, in order that they may reach for full human dignity.

That's great, of course. Except that he turned words over to ordinary, ignorant people as though words could be used as valuable weapons in one's own personal struggles. That got him into trouble. His friend Ivan Illich, also a well-known educator, put it this way:

> The Brazilian teacher Paulo Freire . . . discovered that any adult can begin to read in a matter of 40 hours if the first words he

decipher are charged with political meaning. Freire trains his teachers to move into a village and to discover the words which designate current important issues, such as the access to a well or the compound interest on the debts owed to the *patron*.[4]

When the villagers c me together in the evening for literacy training, their discussion focuses upon these key words. "They begin to realize," Illich explains, "that each word stays on the blackboard even after its sound has faded. The letters continue to unlock reality and to make it manageable as a problem. I have frequently witnessed how discussants grow in social awareness and how they are impelled to take political action as fast as they learn to read. They seem to take reality into their hands as they write it down. . . . My friend Freire since 1962 has moved from exile to exile, mainly because he refuses to conduct his sessions around words which are preselected by approved educators, rather than those which his discussants bring to the class."[5]

Freire contrasts his educational method with the traditional method, which he calls the banking method, wherein the student piles up information and knowledge bit by bit as it is doled out to him by his mentors. The key word for Freire's method is *conscientization* (from the Portuguese *conscientizacao*). This word combines the meanings of conscience and consciousness, and includes three facets. The new, or awakened, person in Latin America (1) becomes more self-conscious (of individual human dignity and power of decision), (2) becomes more conscious of one's situation (aware of forces that enslave and those that offer hope), and (3) becomes more conscientious (ready to act in a fully human and responsible role). Obviously, there is a similarity to the familiar phrase in North America, consciousness-raising. But Freire and other liberationist educators—and there are parallel roots in the educational philosophy native to the United States—provide a consistent framework and rationale. Their challenge remains before both public and church educators in the United States today.

Look again at the threefold definition of conscientization in the previous paragraph. Would not these be good goals for education for lay ministry? And look again at Freire's adult literacy method. Would not this be a good method—adapted, of course—for education for lay ministry?

Reformation and Liberation

How does this "new" theology relate to traditional theologies? I could have drawn these same theological points out of our native scene, using familiar but minority traditions within Christian churches in America. Instead I described liberation theology as from afar—South America, even with Marxist overtones. Now I believe that I am in a position to claim that liberation theology, even in an exotic form, is basically compatible with mainline Reformation traditions. There are differences of emphasis, of course, but this has always been true. Fundamentally, liberation theology offers a fresh and helpful way to apply mainline traditions to contemporary life. It also provides a useful focus for the lay ministry of Christians in America today.

Incidentally, were I Roman Catholic—as most Latin American theologians are—I would be drawing these same connections with the theology emerging from Vatican II. Other Catholics also have important connecting links. And, obviously, were I an inheritor of the radical or left-wing Reformation tradition (Baptists, Friends, Brethren, etc.) I would claim a direct and explicit connection with modern liberation theology. The themes are biblical and universal.

From the mainline Reformation perspective there can be no argument with making freedom a major category within Christian experience and theology. Luther's emphasis upon

Christian liberty—that the Christian man is the most free lord of all—was virtually the battle cry of the Reformation. Of course, there were hundreds of differing interpretations of that cry and the sixteenth-century movement quickly splintered.

However, there would also have been little argument with making liberation a correlate of freedom. In other words, nearly everybody would have agreed that in the name of freedom some serious and fresh liberating needed to be done. In this context the very word Protestant—meaning both protest and firm affirmation—implies liberation. A stress upon the priesthood of all believers was intended to liberate the lay Christian from a slavish obedience to a priest. And the idea of every Christian fulfilling a calling, each in one's own life situation, had the same impact on human dignity.

The problem of connections comes with varying historical interpretations. Let me touch upon three interrelated themes wherein criticisms have been leveled at the new liberation theology: (1) God both in and above human history, (2) the relation between redemption and general history, and (3) theological methodology.

God Both In and Above

Liberation theologies, some critics claim, are so intent upon identifying God at work in human history and involved in bringing change to the economic and political systems, that God is effectively confined to these areas. His otherness, beyondness, independence, or transcendence are virtually lost or rendered meaningless. This is the same charge leveled at an earlier liberal theology that overemphasized God's immanence, or indwelling presence, at the expense of his transcendence.

It is true that the liberalism of the early twentieth century tended to find God within the world and its processes and programs, identifying God and Christianity with the best in human society and culture, and seeing the United Nations as forerunner of the coming world community which will become the kingdom of God. Liberals emphasized *continuity* between God and his creation, Holy Spirit and human spirit, Christ and other human beings, God's work and human endeavor, God's kingdom and human social programs. In reaction there emerged in the mid-twentieth century a neo-orthodoxy, with renewed Reformation roots, which stressed that God is transcendent, above and beyond his creation; quite different from or wholly other than humanity, alien to the processes of nature and human reason, and known only as he breaks in or intrudes himself by revelation.

It would be possible to claim that neo-orthodoxy speaks for the Reformation and that liberation theology perpetuates liberalism. But in actual fact, all four of these theologies at their best (let me name Karl Barth, Martin Luther, Gustavo Gutierrez, and John Bennett) either maintain a careful balance of immanence/transcendence or assert the irrelevance of such a distinction.

The best term to reconcile these ways of thinking is "relevant transcendence." The Reformation spoke of God's Word and personal address. Personal address is always relevant transcendence—a word from "out there" which addresses you, and involves you "in here." Though God speaks from on high, his Word has come fully among us. Though this dialectic, this conversation, always leaves human beings overcome, yet the conversation continues. And the involvement is total. That Word has shocking relevance for the totality of life and, indeed, for this whole world. This Word is not a foreign object stuck down into this earth, a kind of pipeline to another world. It is relevant, pertinent to all of life, a new dimension added to every aspect of life.

Several decades ago Dietrich Bonhoeffer, martyr under the Nazis, spoke of the "worldliness" of Christianity and insisted that

God's transcendence is this-worldly, so that our relation to God is not a religious relation to a supreme being, but a new life for others, "a participation in the Being of Jesus for others."

The best-known liberation theologians also maintain this balance. After all, that is the meaning of the Incarnation, the major biblical theme which stresses that in Jesus God became fully human and that God is always like that—fully with us and fully among us, while never failing to be God at the same time. He is "the beyond in our midst." No tradition fully preserves a theologian, or any practicing Christian, from imbalance in grasping these matters, and the intention to maintain that balance shows that there is no fundamental quarrel between Reformation and liberation theology.

Liberation theologians would claim that anyone who ignores the vast arenas of economics and politics in shaping a theology has, in effect, deformed or crippled the Incarnation. They would also assert that to find the face of Jesus in the face of the poor does not mean that Jesus is not also God, nor does it reduce God to the faces of people. Instead, liberation theology asserts that one can see God by looking lovingly at the poor, and that the Bible encourages that.

Redemption and Social Justice

A second criticism of liberation theologians is that they fail to distinguish between God's redemption in Christ Jesus and the quest for social justice. This is similar to the first criticism but invokes a different Reformation principle, namely, the doctrine of the two kingdoms.

Ever since Jesus said, "Render unto Caesar the things that are Caesar's and unto God the things that are God's," the biblical tradition has carried this duality of approach to the Christian life. In its Protestant form, this tradition has often been used to maintain a separation between, on the one hand, the gospel as it affects the hearts and lives of individual Christians or the Christian fellowship, and, on the other hand, the way people—including Christians—behave in the larger society. The contrast is between redemption and creation, a contrast between the way one acts in private or spiritual life (perhaps also family and Sunday life) and the way one acts in business, politics, and the public arenas of society.

With this viewpoint liberation theologians are in sharp conflict. They may be in such sharp conflict with an idea so well entrenched that they become unbalanced in the opposite direction of denying any distinction at all. They would point out that the Bible never intended to suggest that the things that belong to Caesar do not also belong to God, but only that taxes are also a Christian obligation, though only a limited obligation, whereas one's debt to God is unlimited.

Furthermore, properly understood, the Reformation teaching about two kingdoms never really intended such a separation but only a distinction. Nor did it really intend to mark out two kingdoms; rather, the purpose was to distinguish two obligations or two kinds of relationship to God, a direct and an indirect. On the one hand, regardless of one's position among human beings, one has a direct relation with God. Here the activity and the authority are wholly on the side of God. Here is the gospel in which people are wholly dependent upon God. In the other relationship God acts through human instruments, and one's relation to God is indirect, through the blessing or chastisement, the nurture or governance of other people.

These are not separate kingdoms. God rules in both these relations, and each person is in active relation to God in both ways throughout the totality of his/her life. The distinction is important to make it crystal clear that salvation belongs wholly to God's initiative in Christ Jesus. But there is no slight excuse in this doctrine for Christians to exclude or ignore their responsibilities under God in any arena such as economics and politics, even though their actions may take justice as the norm rather than love.

It is interesting to see how, in the best known volume in English from South American liberationists, *A Theology of Liberation,* Gustavo Gutierrez carefully distinguishes three meanings of the term *liberation.* In the first place, he asserts, liberation "expresses the aspirations of oppressed peoples and social classes, emphasizing the conflictual aspect of the economic, social, and political process which puts them at odds with wealthy nations and oppressive classes." At a second and deeper level, he adds that liberation "can be applied to an understanding of history. Man is seen as assuming conscious responsibility for his own destiny." On the third and deepest level, Gutierrez affirms, "Christ is presented as the one who brings us liberation. Christ the Savior liberates man from sin, which is the ultimate root of all disruption of friendship and of all injustice and oppression. Christ makes man truly free; that is to say, he enables man to live in communion with him; and this is the basis for all human brotherhood."[6]

Then he insists that these three levels are all part of a single, complex process "which finds its deepest sense and its full realization in the saving work of Christ."[7] He elaborates these, much as I have done with the two-kingdoms doctrine, by distinguishing but refusing to separate.

From my perspective as a Lutheran, Gutierrez does not take enough pains to stress that salvation is by God's initiative—i.e., by faith alone—but this is because he is thoroughly Roman Catholic, not because he is a liberation theologian.

The Method Defended

Some traditional theologians criticize liberation theologians, in the third place, because the latter group stresses an action/reflection model of doing theology, drawing insights from their own specific context, and seeing direct connection with biblical events and stories. This, the critics claim, is too subjective with too limited a set of political and social conditions for creating theology, when there should be a more universal, objective claim.

One can, as I have hinted earlier, attack traditional methodology for being badly biased itself. Here it will be more helpful to point out that the method of liberationists has been broadly used in the Christian tradition and that no theology can be objective or in itself universal.

No matter how scientific a theologian tries to be, theology emerges from the Christian community and that community's faith. Faith always has a subjective element. It always roots affectively in personal and group experiences. After all, one does reflect best upon those matters with which one is actively engaged. Pietists may overplay personal, pious experience. Catholics may unduly exalt church authority. Scholastic Protestants may cling too closely to propositions like "justification by grace through faith." Liberationists may draw too heavily on instances of economic injustice, though that condition itself is surely as widely experienced as the others. All can and do find the experiences that they prize modeled in Scripture, though some will use that correlation—between what they experience and what the Bible tells—as their authority more than others will. In any case, the Bible is a shared memory of images for all Christians who will seek to relate those images to their daily pilgrimage.

Without doubt, it is helpful for professional theologians to bring as much objectivity and scientific scrutiny as possible to bear upon the material of faith with which they work. There is, however, no universally recognized way to do this, beyond certain broad categories of honesty and coherence. What can be done and must be done is to keep a variety of theologies in dialogue and mutual correction within one world of Christian discourse.

Inevitably, a theologian's life-setting, church experience, and cultural milieu give shape to her/his theology. The whole study of historical theology assumes that in certain ages and at particular places theologians will choose words and circulate images that are somewhat different because of the circumstances. Most frequently it has been the philosophy of the day that has involved theologians and shaped their formulations. Here liberationists add a corrective word, "You dare not ignore the way your economic condition (poverty or wealth) and your politico-economic ideology shape your theological work." Traditional theologians reply, also correctively, "You must refine the philosophic implications of your theology—especially if you're going to use those tricky Marxist philosophies."

Robert McAfee Brown, noted North American Protestant, has forcefully made the point about a dialogue of theologies in an article called "Context Affects Content: The Rootedness of All Theology."[8] His first statement is that all theologies are contextually conditioned. His second is that there is nothing wrong with that, since such human embodiment of Christian thought is part of the Word being made flesh. He goes on to indicate how doing theology in an ecumenical age will involve the give-and-take of many indigenous theologies. Each can help the others to see the time-bound and limited features of their own formulations, and each can find correction of its own bias through participation in dialogue on the broadest possible scale.

What Is Your Theology?

I have described liberation theology, indicating that there are many liberation theologies. I have shown that they differ with traditional theologies in emphasis rather than absolute contradiction, and I have ended with the suggestion that it will be best for the worldwide church if there is a healthy dialogue among various Christian theologies.

I am not advocating that the reader adopt the Latin American version of liberation theology. Nor must the reader contribute directly to the world's theological dialogues. This will be done mostly by formally trained theologians in universities and seminaries. On the other hand, formal theologians should certainly draw carefully upon the insights of lay people who are committed to a weekday ministry as these theologians build their formulations out of the life of the church. I have already indicated at the end of chapter 4 that I believe the coming age of Christian theology (contrasted with earlier ages) should be one impelled by the needs of the *laos,* or whole People of God, to *be* the Church *in* the world. I certainly think there should be a strong note of liberation in it, and I am urging in this volume that there be a strong note of liberation in your personal theology as well.

What is your theology? You have to develop and live out your own theology, impelled by your own needs as one Christian trying to be a part of the church in the world.

How do you develop an adequate theology? Probably we could better speak of a philosophy of life. It's not like building a shed with a few boards you pick up. You can't just decide to select a few doctrines, lean them against each other, and pound in a few nails. Nor do you go to your parents or pastor, ask them for a theology, and just live with that. The process is more organic and involves something of both these procedures. As we grow we come to awareness with many impressions and ideas already deeply embedded, a lot of them from parents and other authority figures. As our thought processes mature we become selective, seeking some consistency while cultivating those images and convictions and explanations of our world that seem to fit for us.

As we increasingly strive to become coherent Christians, we

study the Bible, we participate in Christian education and worship, and perhaps we read some theology. Then we try to fit all this in with everything else we are learning and experiencing. We never get rid of inconsistency. Puzzles are unresolved; mystery surrounds some areas of our thought/experience; conflicts remain. We are both sinners and people of faith. Our commitment to our culture does not always mesh with our commitment to Christ. Are we peddling seeds of dynamite? Are we part of the establishment, or are we committed to the underground consciousness-raising liberators? Can we really live in One World, or are we for all practical purposes limited to our own neighborhood or nation?

A pattern or style of daily commitment and action has emerged or will emerge in your life. This is your practical, working theology. In this volume I am urging that you work out pieces of this pattern in dialogue and mutual support with fellow Christians right at those places of daily association. You will realize that this description of how your theology develops is similar to—and indeed blends with—the description of decision-making in the next chapter. Theology and ethics, or thought and action, are two parts of the same whole.

In some such way formal theology will seep into your life, partly through the general life of the church, and partly through your own study. It may provide a broad framework for your thought. However, let us now take a closer look at the way one goes about living the Christian life and taking up ministry in the weekday world.

Chapter Six

How Liberated Lifestyles Take Shape

Lifestyle and Ministry

Images like "liberator" and "lay ministry" are still quite vague. They cannot be pinpointed for you in a book. Nor can your pastor make your assignment for you.

"The pastor," says John Schramm, "is one who equips people for their ministry and one who, then, participates with them in it." But the action will probably be where those people are *themselves* most involved. Schramm adds:

> As a pastor in the Community of Christ, this was very difficult for me to learn to do. Perhaps an illustration will communicate the point. A very capable woman kept saying for nearly a year and a half: "Be my Bishop; give me my assignment; put me on a committee." I had almost given in when she conceived of an idea called "Home Buyers." Since that time thirty-five families have moved into their own homes which they are now in the process of buying—because of one woman. She found her ministry instead of having me assign her one.[1]

A lay person will have to find her or his own niche. It's a matter of individual gifts and talents, a matter of circumstances and job, a matter of desire and personal decision. It is also a matter of call and the inspiration of the Holy Spirit.

One's ministry may channel energies mainly into a particular enterprise, like the Home Buyers above, or into the cultivation of a particular gift or skill—like daily counseling or grass-roots political action. Or one's ministry may be much broader, simply a lifestyle that pervades one's whole existence.

Roy Blumhorst does not even like the phrase "lay ministry" because time is wasted trying to define it in relation to clergy ministry, or in trying to package it for types and groups.

> I prefer to treat ministry as more of an adverb. The servanthood which I have received from Christ influences the *way* I approach everything about my life. I live my life in many places, doing many things, among many people. My ministry is to constantly be integrating what's going on in my life with what I believe and value as a Christian. If I am a pastor, I will have to intersect faith and pastoring. If I am also a father, then fatherhood and faith must intersect. If I belong to a congregation, then participation in the congregation and faith intersect. In fact, there is really no part of my life which is excluded from the lens . . . of ministry.[2]

Nonetheless, there are some helpful background things to say by way of interpretation and illustration, whether lay ministry is a particular enterprise or a comprehensive lifestyle, though for most people it will be both.

The Peculiar Dimension

First of all, we must remind ourselves that both lifestyle and ministry come from within a person. They are the outcome of natural expression of the Christian's basic being. Furthermore, there is a peculiar dimension to the life of the Christian because of what God has done for us in Christ and what Christ is doing within us. Paul used a number of illustrations to depict this new situation and new life. It is like enemies who have been reconciled and become friends. It is like the stranger who has been adopted and given sonship in a family. It is like the dead person brought to life again, like the cut-off tree limb grafted back onto the tree, or like the unclean person who is washed and made clean.

But one of Paul's strongest images is freedom. The Christian experience is like the slave who is purchased and then redeemed or emancipated, like a debtor forgiven the debt and released from that burden. In Galatians he declares, "For freedom Christ has set us free" (5:1) and, "You were called to freedom, brethren" (5:13).

This means that the Christian is freed from selfishness and self-serving. Not completely, of course, because one remains a sinner, but no longer a slave to sin and selfishness. Christians have been given the ability to live by resources that lie beyond themselves. It is the good news that we are being cared for and that our salvation has been given to us while we are still sinners.

After all, we're human beings who rebel against God and try to make it on our own. We try to justify ourselves; we strain to get ahead in an endless rat race. Eagerly we grasp for elusive success. Anxiously we stoke a furnace of pride. We're always intent on taking care of number one. But God tells us to relax, to trust Christ, and to accept the good gifts of divine grace in faith. That will bring deep freedom. You won't have to worry, and you don't have to strive when it comes to the most important things, the ultimates of salvation and eternal life.

That doesn't mean that life will now be crowned with all kinds of success. Rather, the Christian now knows that on one's own one will fail. One is moved to surrender, and to look beyond oneself for the good life. Not that the Christian always surrenders and always trusts when confronting other people in daily work and common associations. One works, and sometimes one struggles and fights. But the desperation—the curse or the sting—is taken out of these battles and the frequent failure, simply because salvation does not hinge upon these efforts. We are free to be unselfish because God has already taken care of us.

From such relaxed freedom comes a deep inner poise, an internal balance. This is the peculiar dimension in the Christian's existence. Because God's grace is a free gift, one is no longer anxious, insecure, or unstable inside. One has poise and confidence. Not being preoccupied within, a person can openly and freely devote full attention to what is going on in the surrounding world. One's energies are freed up for the demands made by external circumstances.

Let's compare the Christian life to the experience of ice-skating. When one first gets up on those clumsy, dangerous skates, ankles wobble, confidence disappears, blades are slippery, the ice is hard, and the distance down is great. A person suddenly has to devote all efforts toward maintaining balance. One will grab other people to keep from falling. That is the graceless person. Months later, after much practice, the experience of getting onto ice skates is entirely different—like taking on wings. Why? Because now your balance is something you can confidently assume as given. Even when you fall you consider it a technical slipup, and you soon regain your confidence. That is the grace-filled person. God gives us our balance. Freed from fear and anxiety about our own security, we are given a deeper security or poise.

Poise like that generally helps one to be useful and capable. Within the chain of authority at the office, in the political party, or in a voluntary association, one can more readily serve the purposes of the enterprise without warping all efforts toward getting ahead by pleasing the boss or gaining popularity. In a position of leadership one can more readily take responsibility without misusing power for one's own aggrandizement. In an emergency one is free and confident enough to do the needed thing—use physical force or tell a joke—even if it startles everyone.

I shall never forget my uncle's ability to say a tension-relieving word in the hayfield. We were working hard to get the hay in before the rain arrived. There was a lot of my uncle's money involved, and some of us were trying too hard. "Oh well," he chuckled, as he worked at top speed, "it's all just for fun!" A touch of humor at the right time can be both a sign of faith and an appropriate service.

In First Thessalonians (chapter 5) Paul calls Christians "children of the day" and contrasts them with the children of the night. The moods of the night, Paul mentions, are sleep and drunkenness. Someone has pointed out that these are the moods of complacency and hysteria. In this sense many Americans are children of the night, and the American public frequently swings back and forth between these moods. For a long time the public is swung high upon the side of complacency and apathy. Then some incident—a crime, a severe shortage, a blackout, a new and shocking statistic—will arouse the media and the people so that the mood shifts swiftly, swinging down from complacency and up into hysteria for a period, until the pendulum moves the other way again. Christians are daylight creatures who can keep their feet on the ground. They work calmly and steadily at the problems of our society without succumbing to the shifting moods of public opinion.

Dag Hammarskjöld, one-time Secretary General of the United Nations, was a good example of one who had an inner poise resulting in a strength and wisdom that served well the peace of the nations. In his position he needed calm objectivity and steady dedication to the elusive cause of peace. He once stated in a speech, "We all have within us a center of stillness surrounded by silence." Personally Dag had reserved that center for the God known in Jesus Christ. From that inner commitment, mostly hidden from public view, issued a life that was strenuously dedicated to the service of humanity.

We are probably not called to such greatness. But we are

called to service. Our freedom and that inner dimension of poise are given to us in order that we can effectively serve God and those around us. "For though I am free from all men," Paul asserted (I Corinthians 9:19), "I have made myself a slave to all." Luther put it in a tight paradox. "A Christian man is the most free lord of all," yet the Christian is at the same time "the most dutiful servant of all."

The Christian life flows readily as the response to the good news of the gospel and the trusting acceptance of God and his good gifts. It is a life of gratitude and loving service to fellow human beings. At the same place where Paul asserts, "for freedom Christ has set us free," he also uses the phrase "faith working through love" (Galatians 5:1, 6). "Faith working through love" well summarizes the Christian life. Or the lay ministry. The Christian life and our lay ministry (in the broadest sense) are simply whatever we do for Christ's sake to answer the most pressing needs of our neighbors, and our neighbors are all humankind.

Another good Pauline way of expressing the same understanding of Christian life and ministry is that of the imitation of Christ (Ephesians 5:1). The peculiar dimension is Christ's own life taking shape within us by the power of the Holy Spirit. It is not only a matter of what Christ has done for us but also what he is doing within us. The shape of his life becomes the shape of each Christian's life. We are to have Christ's mind who emptied himself, became a servant among human beings, and obediently died on a cross. Therefore, God has raised him up and exalted his name above every name (Philippians 2:5-11).

That is the shape our lives are to take, the "swoop of grace" bending down to serve human need, obedient even to death, hoping that God will then raise us up to a new life. The Christian life reenacts the servant-shape of Christ's coming among human beings. There is an endless flow of imitators of Christ throughout the centuries, in endless variations as each differs from the others in the person, the gifts, and the circumstances within which the arc of Christ's coming is realized.

Reaching Decisions

How then does one develop one's own lifestyle and ministry? We all imitate Christ; we all carry the peculiar dimension of Christian freedom and poise. Ours is the servant-shape. Yet each has a unique lifestyle and a particular ministry. How do we make the right decisions for our own lives?

From the perspective of decision-making, the freedom, poise, and servant-shape are all a readiness. The decision itself emerges in the discovery of a neighbor's need and an uncovering of what it takes to meet that need. The Christian's lifestyle is a movement between the two poles of faith and neighbor love. The Christian's ministry is in stretching oneself between the servant-shape of Christ and the human facts that describe some significant human need. The Christian action is in outfitting oneself responsibly to meet a need. This means you must get the facts. To be responsible is to be well informed. To act fittingly is to be keenly aware of what is going on. With the disciplined awareness of a good servant you anticipate where your ministrations will be needed most, and you fit yourself into that scene and that action.

If God's grace provides our balance, and the servant-shape determines our stance, then the appropriate action emerges from the circumstance. Just so the boxer who takes a characteristic and balanced stance adjusts his footwork and punching to the specific moment-by-moment actions of his opponent.

By no means does this imply that the Christian acts out of whim or the intuition of the moment. One must accumulate the facts and interpret them wisely. To some extent one must become an interpreter of the times, able to spot trends, find hopeful openings, and discern God's hand in the events. Activist church members who adopted slogans like "Go where the action is," and "Let the world set the agenda" were in the right to have seen that strategy and decision-making were formed out of a grasp of the basic movements that shape the age. Jesus once said "My Father is working still, and I am working" (John 5:17). That should be the cue to the modern Christian's ministry. Find out where God is moving in the life about you and take action that fits God's action.

We have already indicated that the revolution of rising expectations carries with it something of God's modern thrust. The drive for liberation is a central carrier of meaning for the Christian's ministry today. Of course, it's not quite that simple. A lot of interpreting remains to be done. Much of it will have to be done by a particular person in a particular situation. Nor can anyone ever discern with utter clarity God's intention for all of humanity, or even for one specific life. Mystery will always remain. We act in faith, not certainty, just as we receive grace by faith.

How then do we reach decisions? Placed at a tension point between faith and a neighbor's need, do we stand alone and without resources? Of course not. Many resources are built into us as human beings. We use commonsense, reasoning powers, and intuition. Social wisdom (and at least some social nonsense!) has been packed into us through our education and previous experience. These are useful resources out of God's creation. Equally important, we never stand alone. Beyond our built-in resources there are possibilities for help that lie beyond ourselves. Let me mention four.

The first is a sharpened biblical perspective. We can study the Bible. We can do that with a particular decision in mind or in order to deepen our perception of God's way of working with his creatures. Any Christian has a working theology. It may turn out to be crude and unbiblical, or it may be essentially sound. In any case it needs constant testing and clarifying—both from experience and from theological or biblical study.

For example, how do you understand what God is? What does it mean to say that the world is his creation? (Incidentally, we also have to question seriously the use of the masculine pronoun "he" in English to describe God.) What is a human being from the biblical perspective? If we wish to respond to God's actions in the modern world as they touch our daily lives, how do we respond to God and not to the sinful manipulations of human beings, since they also impinge on every event in our experience? We need to turn to Bible study and the works of theologians as resources for our own functioning perspective.

The second resource is decision-making in the church itself, both in its long history and as a contemporary community. Here are many and varied strategies and a vast arsenal of tactics for Christians facing the vexing problems of human life and society upon this planet.

Very few explicit directives will emerge from a study of the church's centuries-long struggle with human societies. There are almost no laws that can govern a Christian's decision-making at a particular point. Again, what church history provides is a balanced perspective that frees one from the confines of time and place. By such study one becomes a better conservative, able to discern what is truly worth conserving over the centuries. And one becomes a better radical, able to uncover the real roots in an effort toward significant change.

Keeping in touch with the church also inspires loyalty and enables one to become part of a larger corporate enterprise. The contemporary church—especially within one's own tradition and denomination—provides opportunites for becoming well-informed, relevant, and helpful in company with a significant band of fellow-workers in the Lord's vineyard. There are many areas of contemporary, even daily, life wherein modern church people have spoken and written with helpful instruction for Christian decision.

We are talking about guidelines—not rules or laws or commandments. Since one must respond personally to God's action as expressed in the events of one's life, no rigid formulation is adequate. On the other hand, it is not enough to say, "Love God and do as you please," or "Take the servant-shape and move out to meet your neighbor's need." There should be guidelines. The church, thinking together, can provide strategies for particular decades and particular parts of the world. There is need for "middle axioms," such as the call for special efforts to overcome racism in America (or South Africa) in the late twentieth century. Obviously, I believe that a crucial contemporary strategy calls for Christians to be liberators and to support liberation movements wisely and vigorously. In the next chapter I'll seek to spell this out a little further.

As a third resource, we must not overlook or underestimate the significance of the other responsible groups to which we belong. For many of us God has set us in the midst of a family. This means that family obligations are already a commitment influencing how we act. This also means that others are to be consulted seriously in any decisions that impinge upon family life. We are citizens of a nation, and we must respond to God's will as it finds partial expression in our duties as citizens and in our national life. Many of us are professionals who must take our profession seriously while listening to the voices of colleagues. Or we belong to other social institutions that lay claim to our loyalty. Since we are free, we need not be subservient to any of these groups; besides, all of them carry some of the twisting effect of sin. But since we are responsible creatures of God and these institutions also carry his good gifts of creation, we give them a voice within our own thinking and find resourceful input into our decision-making.

The fourth needed resource for the best Christian decision-making is a personal support group. It may draw heavily on one or more of the relationships already mentioned—congregation, family, political unit, or profession. But it will be more ad hoc or intimate—a chance to bounce your thinking off of people who know you and are concerned with you. It may be that such help comes more readily from a series of individual counseling sessions. One simply needs to test one's thinking, conscience, intuition, and conclusions with the responses from other people.

None of this yields the decision. Given the servant-stance and all these resources, one's primary attention is still centered upon the need of one's neighbor, the facts that surround that need, and the interpretation of contemporary events. One final aspect of decision-making needs to be mentioned: through this network of needs/facts/interpretation, the Holy Spirit leads the Christian to the right decision. This may be a sudden and convincing intuition, or it may be a gradual, sweated-out conclusion that grows stronger. It may seem like the culmination of a lot of garnered advice, or it may result in a risky, unlikely seeming choice. In any case, it will be reached by a combination of studied investigation and openness to the Spirit's leadership.

This is not to say that all Christian decisions are deliberate and agonizing. Habits, routines, established commitments, and spontaneous acts of service all play a large role in the lifestyle of the Christian. Any worthwhile ministry has its well-established patterns. But at times crucial decisions are forced upon us, and at regular intervals we need to reassess carefully the routines in which we find ourselves.

Let me summarize. God sets us free to serve. We are given in Christ a servant-shape for our life and ministry. As resources we have a biblical perspective, the Christian community for strategy and teamwork, and supportive human communities. Bringing all these to bear upon the circumstances that surround the specific needs we seek to serve, we reach our decisions by the inspiration of the Holy Spirit as that Spirit shows us how God is at work within those circumstances.

A friend of mine tells this parable of Christian decision-making in the face of one of today's toughest issues. A small, traditional country is so economically precarious that a minority party has won power, backed by a nearby colossus of a nation with overwhelming military might and an ideology hostile to the Christian church. It is clear that the country is facing repressive totalitarian rule. The men and women of the theological faculty at the leading university are gathered for their last closed-door session. They know each other well, and, after intense prayer, they face their situation. It is agreed that some of them will have to collaborate rather completely in order to keep the possibility of theological training alive. Others will remain on the faculty as long as possible while quietly supporting the underground resistance movement—helping refugees to escape and keeping the flame of resistance alive. A third group will disappear now into the service of that underground. One or two will flee to safe countries to secure support for the about-to-be persecuted church.

They agree that all will be faithful to their Lord, and loyal to their Christian faith. Each agrees to trust all the others. Then, since these new circumstances require brand-new roles for everybody, they draw straws to see which persons take up which tasks.

The Holy Spirit *can* work through the drawing of straws. God can work in many other marvelous ways too. More often, though, the Spirit works through mundane, even routine, channels, the ones that also require wise decisions on our part.

Tom, aged thirty-two, faces a career choice. He has always had a strong sense of calling. As a student he got an excellent liberal arts education with a strong concentration in economics. His social conscience propelled him into leadership in voluntary, interracial welfare agencies, and he had rather assumed that he would become a staff member for such an organization, or a lay missionary bringing economic skills to overseas service. Temporarily, he took a research job with a large corporation in his city. Suddenly, in a turnabout of the corporate leadership, he became head of the research division. Tom is startled by the influence his suggestions carry among the ten division heads. This is an exhilarating experience. The company's decisions affect the worldwide production and distribution of foodstuffs. It could be a great opportunity for ministry.

There are dangers in this turn of Tom's career. Pure power politics could crush him. The company may decide he is disloyal if his desire to help overcome world hunger appears to distort his research and the decisions required by a profit-making corporation. He does not know whether personal fulfillment is possible within the tensions of the corporate executive's life. However—for the present—he and his Christian support group find in this surprising opening the work of the Holy Spirit intertwined with a careful, even agonizing, decision.

Dave thought he was headed into the ordained ministry. But some parts of seminary education made him wonder. Finally, he simply gagged at the Greek requirement. Meanwhile, he enjoyed his field education opportunities, which consisted of assisting probation officers, and he began to envision a career in social work. But this required another degree; meanwhile, finances pressed him into public school teaching. After several years that were low in terms of direction, and even in specific church identificaton, he found himself in special education providing help for the blind and the visually handicapped.

Fairly suddenly, rather surprisingly, his enthusiasm for "main-streaming the handicapped" took a surge, his skills were remarkably well fitted to his tasks, and he found a wave of support for the new programs he was building. Even the people of his congregation became resourceful supporters. The Holy

Spirit had handed him an unusually rich ministry. Of course, he had been searching for it through some trying years.

Usually such decisions about lay ministry include more than a matching of skills with jobs under the guidance of the Holy Spirit. One is also interpreting life and what is happening in our universe.

As an architect, Norman has the opportunity to bring his Christian understanding of our world to bear upon his daily decisions. His sense of calling leads him to try to work in such a way that, as expressed in a Vatican II document, "the world may be fashioned anew according to God's design and reach its fulfillment." That kind of goal often puts him into conflict with clients who will settle for much less in the buildings they want. For example, his commitment to truth causes him to deplore "deceits, affectations, artificialities, and insincerities." Clients are shocked when he rejects plastics and a host of imitative materials. Norman spends a lot of time trying to persuade people that his concern for integrity also makes good sense for their investment.

An architect is an artist, and Norman believes "that art is probably the only human enterprise which can say something directly about the existence of that category of religious experience we call the holy." But a real work of art takes time and money. For Norman, "The pressure to sacrifice the artistic values of design to those which can be measured in cost is nearly constant."

> When people talk about an artist's suffering they really refer to the tortures of decision and sometimes remorse that often accompany this problem. The Christian architect (and the non-Christian as well) knows that his faithfulness in this concern is the most valuable gift he can make to the world.

He feels that there are other large questions which shape the Christian architect's daily decisions.

How can he witness, through the expressive character of his architectural project, to his faith in an orderly universe, to an order which is often so clouded as to seem absurd? How can a building be an echo of the gospel with its creative liberating character? What is the nature of form which reflects the grace and relentless kindness of God's love? What kind of spaces and shapes and colors and textures and visual rhythms say something about the Christian's faith that the Holy Spirit is active, that the work of God is continuing?[3]

Evangelism Too

But, someone will ask, why do you not speak of evangelism as a part of the contemporary lifestyle and ministry? Let me reply, I *am* speaking of evangelism. All that I have stated in this chapter (and will say about the church's service in the next chapter) could come under the heading of evangelism and is concerned with "winning people for Christ." It certainly assumes that the right word, or "speaking for Christ," will be said when opportunity offers. To look at one's life and work as ministry is the basis of evangelism. The last of Norman's questions (above) deals with redemption and is directly evangelistic in intent. The workbench *can* be a distribution center for the spread of the good news of God's grace.

There is a receptionist for a large business enterprise whose steady good cheer in the face of pressures and trying circumstances provides a lift for many of the individuals in the flow of humanity passing her desk. In other circumstances we would easily speak of her witness as an inspiration. There is the government clerk who day in and day out listens to complaints as his daily work. The only choices he can exercise are in the way he puts these requests to his superiors. Yet he steadily maintains faith in people, and struggles for a positive, or humane, formulation of the public's grievances. There is the elevator operator in a hospital who hums a familiar hymn tune of reassurance as he takes patients and their fears up to the operating room. Let's not forget the special duty nurse who, during loving assistance through lengthy illnesses, often presents a convincing evidence of Christian faith. Then there is the businessman whose unfailing pleasure in human relationships extends to everyone around him and proves contagious. Perhaps some consider him fatuous, but there is a lot of evidence that many people have been helped. All of these individuals see more to life when viewed in the light of Jesus Christ, and thus help others to see more to life. That is witness, and that kind of living is the only proper context for a specifically evangelistic word. It is when people are seriously addressing any of the whole gamut of modern human needs that evangelism can flourish like a naturally growing plant.

We must remember once more that the whole Christian enterprise—worship, social service, evangelism, lifestyle, and weekday ministry—is aimed at reconciling human beings and all of humanity to God. It is all a part of the good news that we have been reconciled to God through Christ, and are made into agents of that reconciliation (II Corinthians 5:18-20). The question is: How does that happen? Or: How do we become effective agents?

I want to suggest that effective agents adapt to the age. This does not mean simple conformity. In fact I have already pointed out that Christians are being called to go against the stream of the culture increasingly in the decades ahead. But this effort to adapt to the way God is working today does involve shaping one's witness to the way people experience life at any time and place.

Paul had this kind of adaptability in mind when he asserted that "though I am free from all men, I have made myself a slave to all, that I might win the more" (I Corinthians 9:19). He became a Jew to win Jews. He was also as one outside the law to win those outside the law, and as weak to win the weak. "I have become all things to all men, that I might by all means save some" (verse 22). Here we have put this idea in terms of emptying ourselves in order to identify with our neighbor and our neighbor's need.

What is the effective lifestyle for the modern agent of reconciliation? There will be great variety. Yet in contrast with previous ages, the modern age does call for a particular kind of person. Contrasting references to some earlier Christian styles as portrayed in literature will illuminate this point.

Style for This Age

When my son was a youngster, he and I read a book called *The Fighting Shortshop.*[4] It told about an American college boy and his friends spending a summer in pre-Castro Cuba. They worked in a sugar mill by day, played baseball for the company team in the evening, and battled intrigue and sabotage against their company during most of the night hours. I began to wonder when these boys slept. Soon I began to marvel at their constant luck in winning precarious victories against insurmountable odds.

Then I became aware that some*one* was keeping a tight control on all events in an attempt to maintain my excitement at white heat. For me all the fight drained out of the fighting shortstop as he moved woodenly through countless crises, exhibiting superior pluck and skill, and abetted by superhuman (i.e., the author's) control.

Neither my son nor I ever finished the story. We got tired of it for the same three reasons that I get tired of most western movies: (1) The hero is too good. (2) He is too obviously being manipulated by the plot-maker. (3) He is moved about in order to excite me—that is, the author is trying to manipulate me.

Looking for better entertainment, my son and I turned to Merchant's *King Arthur and His Knights.*[5] This was a marked improvement. In this story the author wasn't trying to manipulate us. The reader can sense that this story is not primarily aimed at one's emotions. Clearly this is the kind of material that has inspired Christian people for many generations. Yet it is hard for today's reader to identify with King Arthur's world as described in these romantic tales. The heroes are too sweet, too good, and the plot-maker keeps interrupting the flow. Added to superior pluck is superhuman righteousness, and added to superior luck is abrupt interference by unseen hands.

Consider, for instance, the glowing goodness of Sir Gareth. He was a kitchen lad working amid the pots and pans when he was sent to rescue a damsel in distress. His companion on the road was a fair lady who was sister to the girl held captive. She mocked this boy and said that he smelled of kitchen grease. But he nobly and gently made no reply. Instead, he rescued a nobleman from six bandits and conquered in mortal combat ugly villains. Then, when he was overthrown by an unknown knight, he merely laughed at himself, taking it in good grace.

Of course, the unknown knight turned out to be Launcelot, King Arthur's greatest warrior. So I guess Gareth married the girl who had mocked him, and they lived happily ever after. Realistically, though, any girl would have a hard time of it married to such a perfect husband.

Sir Galahad is still more obvious as an example:

> My good blade carves the casques of men
> My tough lance thrusteth sure,
> My strength is as the strength of ten,
> Because my heart is pure.

Galahad is described as youthful, slim, upright, and very fair. He was brought up in a company of ladies, among everything that is fair and innocent, beautiful as a young tree, pure as snow. When Launcelot sees him he exclaims: "May you be good forever, Sir Galahad, for you are the most beautiful knight I have ever seen." He was dressed in crimson satin, with a mantel of ermine. He was a prince, and all the knights of the Round Table welcomed him to the greatest seat at the table, the Seat Perilous, which had waited empty for him for many years.

It is all too nice and sweet. Furthermore, it is unnatural, and we moderns simply do not care for it. Even the word "noble" is often a bad one in our day, and nobody wants to be called "a knight in shining armor" or "a Sir Galahad."

The other problem with the stories of King Arthur is that the plot never thickens because all problems are quickly resolved by magical acts in behalf of the hero. Mysteriously, a woman's arm rises from the waters of a lake to hold out an invincible sword for the hero's hand. Or a sword imbedded in stone releases itself for Arthur alone, thereby announcing that this lad is to be the king. And the wizard, Merlin, is usually ready with a rescue. How can these characters become anything, much less achieve anything on their own, under such circumstances?

Of course, it would be typical for a modern reader to miss the whole point of these stories, namely, God's grace at work among human beings. For modern people life is flat—even in this space age with distances that let the imagination soar. We live a two-dimensional existence, limited to the here and the now, and circumscribed by the human.

This age cannot picture superhuman graces residing in a human personality. Nor can we see that behind strange doings the hand of God may be at work. Scientists can produce startling and mysterious events, but storytellers should not try. And nobody believes Christians who claim marvelous happenings in human lives.

At any rate, external symbols can hardly point to unseen grace. Who will believe that a magic Round Table can produce noble fellowship? Or who will agree that a fairy's sword in a lad's hand can win God's victories on earth, or that the words and deeds of human beings can be the piercing sword of God's Spirit? Will anyone see actual power for daily existence in a flame-circled Chalice (whether it be the cup of the Lord's Supper or the vision of sacrificial service)?

King Arthur is too kingly. His stories are too well-guided by unseen hands. Today we want more inward, psychological reality for our characters.

If we come closer to our time—say, American Protestantism at the turn of the twentieth century—we find an improvement in this respect. Charles Sheldon's *In His Steps* [6] does not show any interference by magical props. The setting is an ordinary congregation of well-to-do citizens in a midwestern city.

Pastor Henry Maxwell and fifty of his parishioners pledged themselves to ask "What would Jesus do?" in each daily-life experience, and then to seek to imitate their Lord.

Rachel Winslow infuriated her mother by turning down the opportunity to become an opera singer in order to devote her musical talents to revival meetings, and settlement-house work in the city's slums.

Editor Edward Norman eliminated the Sunday edition of the *Daily News,* refused liquor and tobacco ads, did not print stories about prize fights and crime, and directed his editorial comments about politics to the moral issues involved.

President Donald Marsh of Lincoln College, together with Pastor Maxwell, entered into ward politics to try to defeat the relicensing of saloons. So it went. First Church was mightily swayed by the power of the Spirit. There were sharp sacrifices and some defections. The battle against saloons was lost that year because too many professing Christians failed to go to the polls. But the "time must come when the Christian forces in the city will triumph," and Virginia Page was ready to give her large fortune to subsidize a Christian newspaper, and to develop social welfare programs in the slums.

Personal romance continued to triumph for young Christians. Pastor Maxwell's vision of a Christian world living under the banner What Would Jesus Do? became contagious, until he foresaw the dawn of the millenium.

It's an inspiring story. Very romantic. Even sweet. But it does not ring true for our day. Again we feel that the author is trying to bring tears to the reader's eyes and to turn the reader's will, through management of the story's characters. Christians continue to believe that the Holy Spirit can touch human hearts and transform human wills so that decisions are radically changed. But neither non-Christians nor Christians expect clear and dramatic evidence of such changed motives.

Certainly we do not expect sudden Christian commitment to result in major triumphs within a city's life. Today nobody expects a revivalistic crusade, for example, to make a visible dent in the social patterns of the city targeted. We don't expect to see the hand of God moving irresistibly through converted hearts to bring his plot to successful conclusion. Most modern people fail to find any plot at all. Loss of meaning is a major modern malady.

How can we see God's grace at work in the modern world? Not through the Catholic's picture of the church as the possessor of potent mysteries like Table, Sword, and Cup. Nor through the revivalist's vision of the church as a growing band of dramatically upright lives that are Spirit-driven, like the singer Rachel Winslow and the editor Edward Norman.

I do not know how the modern storyteller or novelist can write a Christian story that will manifest God's power in human events so that the whole will appear genuine to the twentieth-century mind. While romance makes good escape reading, literature that would seriously tell about reality must, in our day, use a "realistic" (a familiar, psychologically acceptable) form.

Nevertheless, this question drives home for each Christian: How do *you* picture God's grace at work in the modern world? Each Christian is called to be a witness, to be a sign pointing to what God is doing through Christ in today's world. How do *you* point to that reality?

You could hold up a cup or a sermon or a book that carries supernatural power. You could point to surprising decisions, dramatically changed lives, or upright people. But modern people will scoff. "That's fine romance," they'll say, "but it's too soft and sentimental for me. When I want to live with heroes who are conveniently manipulated for my excitement, I'll read *The Fighting Shortstop* or *Quick Draw McGraw.* Real life isn't like that."

How does the Christian show God's grace at work in the flatland of modern living? The answer is simple, painfully simple. One has nothing to point to, but one has a little something to give: oneself in Christ. One can meet a neighbor's need in love. In any human equation one can throw oneself into the balance on the side of justice or human need.

Not that such self-sacrifice assures the right answer for every equation. There is certainly no promise that people will take notice, that evil will recede, or that social systems will crumble and change. Only occasionally do these things happen.

Yet such all-out, stark identification with the neighbor's need may be recognized as an asset even by a worldly, modern neighbor. Strangely and quietly God moves within such personal encounters to touch human lives even in our own day.

How then, do Christians show God's grace at work? They can't. Each simply *is* a person in Christ and for one's neighbor. Then God will, when he chooses, use that Christian as a sign through which another person sees and receives God's grace. Does that describe a lifestyle? It describes a myriad of lifestyles, all with a common thread.

Three Who Live It

Three illustrations will suffice, all drawn from the world of work. None is offbeat or dramatic; here we are talking about

ordinary people who find a ministry of love and service. One
witness is primarily personal; the other two are more social,
aimed at better services for a broad public—neither emphasis
should be ignored by those interested in Christian lifestyles for
our age.

Cecilia is an experienced nurse. For her, nursing is a way of
life. She has learned to listen to people, showing sensitivity to
moods and needs. More than once she has sensed when an
acquaintance has misunderstood what a doctor has said, and
through listening and reinterpretation she has relieved a
troubled mind of a destructive burden.

Cecilia also finds the attributes of a good nurse to be similar to
the Christian lifestyle: "to have a genuine concern for people,
regardless of their racial and cultural background, education,
state of mind and behavior, personality and attitude, manners
and morals, state of health, cleanliness of body, etc."[7]
Ministering when death hovers near, sharing a unique intimacy
in a bedside relation that involves the whole person, being
dedicated to maintaining a person's dignity and integrity when
these are threatened—for this nurse these are rich opportunities
to love after the manner of Christ's love. Her prayers often are
quick and simple—perhaps heard by the sick one, perhaps not.
Sometimes, however, she finds herself providing faith-support
for an individual whose religion may be very different from her
own, or she helps ease a patient into acceptance of impending
death through words murmured or a gentle holding of hands.

With family and community responsibilities, Cecilia has
learned to limit her professional life to what she calls bouquet
nursing and bottom of the barrel nursing. Instead of sending
flowers for a sick friend she volunteers her professional help for
one or more eight-hour shifts as her bouquet at another person's
time of crisis. She also makes herself available at a nearby
hospital for those times when they have reached the bottom of
their lists for nursing help. Since these are almost always crisis

situations, they offer special challenge in the dimension of caring, making herself intently available at a point of great stress.

One incident typifies her creative love at work. A patient who had attempted suicide through an overdose of drugs lay in a deep coma, unresponsive to therapy. When Cecilia came on duty she was told that there was not much hope for recovery.

> As I cared for her that day, I talked to her from time to time in a quiet voice about one of the Greek Islands in the Aegean Sea which is a favorite place of mine. I suggested that if she were to walk with me up that heather covered hill, we could see the entire island. So I described the feel of the rough textured heather on our legs as we walked through it. I described the color of the heather plants and the pungent fragrance. I tried to convey the feeling of the warmth of the sun and the clear sweet air so characteristic of Greece. I told her of the inhabitants of the island, the little donkeys and peacocks, and how their voices were intermingled with the sea sounds and buzzing of insects. And then we "walked" down the other side of the hill, under the olive trees and onto the white sand, and stood looking out at the incredibly blue sea.
>
> For the first time since her admittance she began to move. Her legs moved in a rhythmic way. Her knee would bend and then the leg extend, and then the other, and they moved alternately. I realized she was "walking."[8]

In time the patient recovered. Sometimes Cecilia wonders whether that woman has any memories of that Greek island.

Richard is a dairy farmer in Pennsylvania where three owners and eleven employees work more than a thousand acres and maintain a herd of three hundred cows. His story is the familiar one of hardships as a youngster on a family farm. While in high school, however, Richard decided to stick with agriculture, even though farming was looked down on as a vocation. "My chief motive," he says, "was a deep feeling that the working and living conditions of the farmers could be and ought to be improved." Later his purposes broadened. Then he "felt a special call to do everything possible in my small corner of the earth to set a modest example of helping to provide food for the world by helping to improve the facilities and methods of the food producer."[9] For Richard these convictions emerged from a sense of responsibility to God as the creator of the universe who gave human beings the earth to till, and from a reading of the Bible which highlights God's intention that people shall not live in need.

Richard has therefore devoted his life to improving his dairy farm as a productive enterprise and a fulfilling place to work. His ministry and lifestyle express themselves in diligence, in wise and progressive concern for production, and in a sustained effort to improve working conditions for farmers—both managers and "hired hands" (who then become respected employees, persons rather than hands). Richard rejoices in the way his farm has pioneered dozens of technical innovations and improvements for dairy farming in his part of the country, in the way his employees make a better living and enjoy a more fulfilling work life, and in the influence for the better which his enterprise has had on the surrounding farms and the country as a whole. He actively works at getting capable young people interested in the arts of animal and soil husbandry, and he even speaks of the role of his farm "in spreading our gospel of human service through soil stewardship and animal husbandry."

Carroll has a more complex way in which he relates Christian commitment to his lifestyle in daily work. He too runs a small business—a public relations firm—but his sense of ministry relates most directly to the difficult area of ethical decisions. There are many moral dilemmas in the wielding of words as a professional in advertising.

Since Carroll believes that "every person and every firm or group has a right and an obligation to describe its purpose for being, its services or products, and the benefits it believes it is bringing or can bring to an individual and society," his firm often agrees to represent unpopular causes or a political candidate who is not likely to win. These are risky decisions for a PR firm which itself depends for business on a good public image. As Carroll puts its:

> We worked for causes which were too controversial for others. We conducted local campaigns for urban renewal, for fluoridation, and for other public issues in elections. We conducted campaigns for statewide issues. We won some and we lost some. We were unpopular with some factions for working with certain causes or with certain candidates. We were berated by those who disagreed with the cause or the candidate, and we were applauded by those who supported them.
>
> But the key factor in all this work was that we always tried to present information in perspective. We sought to deaden rumors not based on fact, to highlight objective information which a voter could hang onto and reason with. . . .
>
> I have come to recognize that those who work in mass communications are to a startling degree frontline troops in the battle of ethical practice.[10]

His work is his ministry. "As a child of God," Carroll points out, "my ministry is to be a creator." Constantly he strives for excellence. Often he acknowledges failure. Frequently he works in tension with a client who would settle for less than excellence, or even less than the truth. Should a particular brochure be an outstanding piece of work, or should it be cheap and mediocre? How does one sense fully what a client's real needs are when the client is willing to accept almost anything "the experts" recommend? When does one turn a client down because one is not quite equipped to meet that particular need? There is such tremendous power in the right choice of words.

> What I can try to do is to go through my workday with a sense of deep conviction about how my job must be done; about the relative importance of doing it consciously as a part of God's creative process; and about the negation I have strewn about when it is done otherwise.[11]

Chapter Seven

Today's Free Styles
—Free Services

A Greedy Goliath

Jimmy Carter is a skilled politician. Jimmy Carter is a responsible President of the United States. Jimmy Carter is a serious evangelical Christian. How much of this third ingredient showed up in his comprehensive energy policy?

If that is too tough a question, ask yourself how much of the Christian ingredient in *you* showed up in *your response* to Carter's energy proposals?

In April of 1977, when Carter made his bold pitch to the American public in unveiling his energy program, he called for conservation and sacrifice in the face of a severe, long-range crisis.

Though this was no new topic, Americans reacted with disbelief. Surely there's some way out; the crisis can't be that extreme. Many leaders said, "Let's try harder, we'll dig and drill and produce more conventional fuels." Overnight, in a third reaction, a variety of special interests pointed out the need for significant alteration of the proposals so that their clients would not get hurt in the shuffle. How did I react? I was secretly glad that I could walk to work, if it became absolutely necessary.

On the day after the announcement, there appeared this headline in Chicago's *Daily News* on an inside page toward the bottom, "Carter Plan Hailed Overseas." The subhead read, "Exit the Greedy Goliath." Keyes Beech wrote from Washington—in his lead before detailing overseas comments—as follows:

> President Carter's energy-saving program is likely to generate more enthusiasm abroad than at home.
>
> It could change the U.S. image from that of a greedy Goliath, consuming 30 per cent of the world's energy with only 6 per cent of its population, to that of a global pacesetter benefiting the rest of mankind by mending its wasteful ways. [1]

Let me use this event to point to three needed ingredients in a contemporary lifestyle, following with three ways in which a liberating church can meet the world's most pressing needs. Thus, this chapter represents a brief fleshing-out of the general descriptions of the church and the Christian in contemporary life, according to my own understanding of God's movement within today's world.

A Lean Lifestyle

Obviously we Americans need to adopt a lean lifestyle, much leaner than most American Christians now practice.

I need not dwell on this because it is a popular theme (for discussion, that is) within our culture. There are a lot of good common-sense reasons—patriotism, bodily health, economic survival during inflation, resistance to consumerism. For some of us older parents our own children with counterculture experience can lead us a long way in this direction. Within the Christian community too the young will probably take the lead.

There are also imperatives for a lean lifestyle which emerge directly from our Christian faith. Traditionally we have agreed that self-discipline is spiritually healthy, that voluntary sacrifice can be ennobling, and that our bodies should be cultivated as effective instruments or as temples of the Lord.

Besides, in these chapters we have been stressing Christian freedom and our call to come out of lesser commitments into a larger commitment to the fellowship and the tasks of God's kingdom which include efforts to move our society toward that kingdom. An extravagant lifestyle threatens that freedom and that service. Not only because of self-indulgence, but, if one's effective service depends on high energy use and a big expense account, one is in a very vulnerable position. Patterns of income and energy use may change rapidly. Probably they *should* change. How well can one adapt? Less use of a comfortable car means less efficiency in business contacts and in visiting friends—either these are lost or one spends more time on them. Are there other ways to do the same things? More importantly, if less energy use and more equitable worldwide distribution of usable forms of energy are moral imperatives for American society today, what will our example and witness be among fellow Christians? Among fellow Americans? Among our fellows throughout the world?

I must be content to leave this issue with only that—the assertion of the need for a leaner lifestyle and a lot of questions. There are too many variables for generalizations. However, let's not face these questions alone, or only during family budget discussions. Our support groups and all of our church structures including our supply trains for liberators, should be wrestling with these questions and forming consensus-decisions when possible.

Maybe lean lifestyle has a second meaning—not only "not fat," but also a style of "leaning against" self-indulgence and the natural assertion of self-interest. For example, in public debate and decision Christians will be ready to resist lobbying efforts that serve their own narrow interests at the expense of broader public policy. Christians will voluntarily take up a lean lifestyle, in both senses of the phrase, and will also more readily accept the constraints placed upon them by wise but burdensome public policies.

As we shall see, a lean lifestyle will also serve the other concerns of this chapter on the world's most pressing needs (most obviously, solidarity with the poor and protest against oppression).

Resistance to Competition

The second way in which Christians should be leading Americans toward a healthier lifestyle is by *resistance to the competitive spirit and system.*

In Bogota, Colombia, some years ago, I met a learned and bearded priest who was now living in one of the poorest shantytowns at the edge of the city. Such shantytowns are numerous around major Latin American cities. In these villages, peasant squatters live in straw huts. They scratch out an existence and hope for a better future for their many children.

This padre teaches in an elementary school. When I asked why, he explained with an illustration. This school does not give each pupil a pencil to use and to take care of. Here pupils take turns caring for all the pencils for the whole class. Each gets a turn to give out, to collect, to sharpen, and to protect.

They are learning to trust each other and to share. Usually such depressingly poor people learn to steal rather than to share. They seldom learn to trust anybody or to take responsibility for one another. That makes all social progress extremely difficult. Sharply competitive school patterns don't help. In fact, cutthroat competition for mere survival is part of the slavery from which they need to be set free.

Great! In the name of Christ this priest is tackling a social problem by devoting his years to the transformation of a few slum kids. He's a humble purveyor of good news.

Of course, I should add that he got his educational ideas through a visit to Mao's China. And alongside his Christian theology, he puts Marxist ideas about class struggle. Obviously, his educational purposes are socialist. Yet fundamentally, he is teaching young people in the name of Christ to trust, to share, and to be free. He believes that only by virtually beginning over again can the societies in the Americas escape the destructive force of harsh competition.

For years as I taught courses in American religious history I would have a class discussion, "How does the devil get his best grip on American society?" My own answer is, through the unbridled spirit of competition, reinforced by our strongest traditions and permeating all the systems of our society. From that standpoint, I would maintain, organized religion in America has served the devil quite well with its fierce denominational competition, its free enterprise for spiritual entrepreneurs, and its success structures for clergy.

There is clearly a broad background for this. For several centuries the leaders of Western civilization have been telling us that a person's freedom lies within oneself, that a person is independent of any higher power, and that one is master of one's own fate. Americans have bought into this deeply (I called it individualism in chapter 4). Now, faced by problems that loom ever larger and more remote from our control, our only answer is to strive harder for the mastery. As a people we become rigid and frantic in asserting that we can win out.

Much of our private living has the same hard self-assertion about it. We must prove to ourselves and to the world that we can rise. We are under the necessity of succeeding. Like the chambered nautilus, we must move from this house and car to bigger ones. We must build up financial security, achieve acceptance and standing in the community, become known for our accomplishments. Our children must be beautiful and sociable. We must feel at least a little superiority over those around us. As one tire ad puts it: "You don't really *need* a tire this good. The new . . . belongs on *your* car, too, if you want above all else *the satisfaction of knowing you are riding on the finest tire that men can make or money can buy.*" A sharp journalist has asserted that a "large part of the drama of daily living consists in working out our plans for proving we are not inferior to anybody."

In a word, for the harried, overactive modern person, success is a compulsion. One must justify oneself in one's own eyes and before the world. Success with its sweet smell is the idol. It is also the taskmaster. Ed Willock in *Ye Gods* points out that

> success is a nice word for something quite nasty. This is most frequently the case when the reference is to financial success or growth in social stature. Success is the thing way out yonder. It is the end that justifies the meanness. It is where the go-getter is going. Success is super-deluxe, A-number-one, free-wheeling PRIDE.[2]

Obviously, this is precisely where the gospel has set Christians free. They are released from that treadmill. As Willock puts it:

> In a game of dog-eat-dog, a Christian is bound to fail by simply refusing to be a dog. In a society where the "devil can take the hindmost" the Christian must choose the tail end. That is the only charitable thing he can do.[3]

Let's clarify that we're not talking about greed, nor simply about sin and selfishness. We're talking about competition as it becomes swollen and unhealthy. In itself the competitive spirit is a good thing, a natural human attribute from God's creation (though this assertion could be contested). Depending on the situation, it may be good or it may be bad to use the competitive spirit. Personally I prefer sharply competitive tennis to the pleasant exercise of volleying the tennis ball back and forth. What is under attack here—as something Christians must resist—is the overemphasis upon competition, the cutthroat nature of much of our competition, the way in which the competitive spirit is nurtured and fostered among us, the unchecked admiration for that spirit and for those who use it to succeed, and the extreme forms through which competition provides patterns of interaction for nearly every institution and arena in which we operate. Too many people get badly hurt, and every one of us experiences some warping of the spirit in such an atmosphere.

Christian lay people are lacerated in such a sharply competitive society. Every effort to live the Christian life weekdays gets smothered at birth. One breathes as a Christian on Sunday and develops other lungs to breathe the sulphurous fumes of competition the other six days.

Listen again to Bill Diehl, whom we met in chapter 4 as the sales manager for a major steel company. Citing studies and his own experience, he points out that the corporate world is a system that stimulates and reinforces "activities related to head and hand," while suppressing "activities related to heart (generosity, compassion, and idealism)." This is not because of especially evil people, for the problem "results from a society based on competition—in business, in schools, in our professions, in sports, in almost everything we do." As Christians we are told that "God accepts us based on whose we are, not what we do." According to Diehl, "To move from Sunday faith to the Monday world, therefore, represents for most lay people, a 180-degree turn in philosophies." Furthermore, Bill believes the clergy fail to understand this. They are aware of many ethical issues in corporate life. Yet clergy do not know that any manager who seeks to relate faith to life finds that "the most important ministry he daily faces is how he can establish in his own division an atmosphere of concern, compassion, healing and love within an institutional environment which rewards performance."[4]

To that I might add that clergy, who are ecclesiastical managers too, ought to be more aware of the oppressive hold which competition has on their professional life. This would simply mean greater sensitivity to our common lot.

Individually, and in our common thought and action, we late twentieth-century Christians are being called by God to develop styles of living and ministries that break with the confining spirit of competition as it presently grips us.

Global Consciousness

The third attribute of a modern and liberated lifestyle for Christians is *global consciousness.* The first two attributes—leanness and resistance to competition—take on a sharper imperative when viewed internationally. And our opening illustration—public reaction to an energy crisis—shows how an overseas perspective (seeing the United States as a greedy Goliath) can help us temper our nationalistic competitiveness and our fat lifestyle with some realism, yielding a broader grasp of the overall situation. Actually, global consciousness is basic to everything stressed in this volume. It is essential for responsible modern living.

In many ways it is forced upon us today. Jim Scherer in *Global Living Here and Now* says:

> In our age, the rest of the world has suddenly become fully *present* to people in North America. We are also *present* to the rest of the world, though perhaps less completely so. The mass media and mass transportation facilities linking the globe have given us the technical means of living, participating and being present in the whole world. Some of the symbols of this revolutionary change are the transistor radio, the TV set, relay satellites and the jumbo jet.[5]

Of course, neither TV documentaries nor packaged tours overseas provide real communication between peoples. That is still difficult. The overwhelming majority of our actual exchanges and vivid personal experiences are limited, contained within a particular geography, with certain types of people, within a certain culture and range of interests. Anything like world brotherhood or sisterhood is only fleetingly experienced at best.

It therefore takes a real effort to think globally at every turn in life. Frequently it is an unpleasant effort. Even though there is a strong American tradition of welcoming into one society immigrants from many lands, and even though there is also a strong American tradition of providing aid for people in calamity or disaster, still we get tired of expressing concern for the miserable millions of this earth, and of facing worldwide issues that are too complex for our comprehension. As Scherer puts its:

> We are a tired and troubled people—tired of criticism, tired of foreign involvements, tired of bearing other people's burdens, tired of maintaining high moral pretenses, tired of saving the world from communism, fascism, hunger and poverty, tired of leadership responsibilities and wanting more than anything else to crawl into our shell.[6]

Let me just say three words in support of a lifestyle that keeps the whole world in view. The first is a how-to suggestion. When the world gets too big and burdensome, reduce it to your backyard and do something about that. All the world's major issues, all the crying needs of peoples across the earth, have direct lines to your own bailiwick. The trick is to see your own daily relationships and tasks in the light of the world situation. Once we are globally aware, we can see that the world's battlelines run right down the street where we live. Then we can join the guerilla fighters behind the barricades in our own backyard (a new use for the old junk pile!). Or, to return to another of our analogies, our compost pile suddenly becomes our best resource for nurturing seeds that will explode into food for the world. Every action we take becomes fraught with implications for worldwide liberation (or oppression).

For more than a decade I have served on the world mission board of my denomination. In this enterprise we know that the gospel evokes a huge human potential movement; our approach to mission tasks is holistic, involving whole persons and the totality of human needs. When we push persistently to the root causes of the problems faced by people elsewhere on the globe, we discover or are told: The thing you can do to best help us is on your own doorstep—change things in the United States. Here at home this involves our politics (for example, as I write, there is a sharp debate about a Panama Canal treaty), our economics (Do our corporations sustain the apartheid system in South Africa?), our racial attitudes (quotas on immigrants and treatment of minorities), our movies (encouraging violence and twisted sexual attitudes), the leading symbols of our culture (Coca-Cola, university degrees, big automobiles), and, indeed, most of whatever else we do (including a sometimes anemic religion). For the members of our world mission board this is a frustrating realization, because all these issues belong in the arenas of other boards of our church, to which we can only refer our concerns. We do not falter in seeking to spread the good news about Jesus Christ, but we return to our congregations with a renewed sense that the crucial action is right here at home.

My second word about global consciousness is this: We Americans badly need to listen to other people and to draw on their strengths for our weaknesses. One experienced speaker about world community says that when he uses the story of the Good Samaritan among American Christians they invariably identify themselves with the Good Samaritan. That is, we assume that we are the strong and helpful ones. He suggests that at some places in the Third World, Americans are identified with the robbers, or those who passed by, or even the innkeeper (well-paid rather than voluntary services). Therefore he stresses that Americans ought, at least at times, to think of themselves as the wounded traveler who desperately needs the ministration of others. Christians should quickly recognize the truth in this point. We need liberation from our affluent, competitive patterns of living. It is part of the style of Christian existence to be open to the spiritual insights and the life experiences of people different from ourselves. God's Word is there to be received, as the words and actions of others repeatedly break in upon our narrow thoughts and feelings.

Let me offer another illustration. In El Salvador, Father Rutilio Grande, recently preached like the Argentine priest described at the very beginning of this book. His people, peasant farmers *(campesinos),* took heart from his message and started to develop a community organization. But the setting is one in which a dictatorial government and a reactionary ruling oligarchy have virtually declared war on the Catholic Church in an effort to maintain repressive power and keep the peasants in serfdom. Father Grande was ambushed and killed. Troops poured into his town of Aquilares, killing perhaps fifty *campesinos* and ransacking all the homes. They claimed to be looking for arms and subversive propaganda. One farm worker stated that the villagers had fortunately already burned everything. "But thank God," he added, "we had even burned the photo of Father Grande. It hurt us deeply but we had to do it." Then he summarized what it all meant to them as Christians:

What we have learned from them is that no one and nothing can take away what we feel. This even strengthens us to see if we are really faithful to the Word of God and to his church of which we form a part. These times and these tests which God sends us shake up the church and take away what is unsure. Only what is really faithful to him and sure of his Word remains. So we should be constant in his Word and in prayer to God so that he will have mercy on his people and grant conviction and repentance to those who persecute the church and torture Christians. This reminds me of when Saul persecuted the church and God granted him conviction and repentance because of the prayer of Christians.

Afterwards he was one of the most fervent apostles in God's apostolate.[7]

Here is a "crucible" experience and a quality of insight from which we Christians in the United States can draw strength for our own tasks and witness.

This second word about global perspectives in Christian lifestyle—namely, that Americans need to listen and receive—connects closely with the description below of the church's service to the world.

My third word about a global lifestyle also connects directly with the following description of the church's service, as one would naturally expect congruence between lifestyle and the forms of the church's service.

The third word is liberation. Without a consistently global perspective one cannot be truly free. Within this volume such a statement is a truism. Yet it needs emphasis. Let me take a two-line ditty and unfold it.

> One World, Two, or Three,
> Which World's Truly Free?

Are there three worlds today? A lot of people think that there are. A First World (with the United States as its hub), a Second World (with Russia as its center), and a Third World. After World War II that kind of thinking roughly matched the political realities. But not today, and it never has made any sense as a description of economic facts or the diffusion of cultures and technology. Where do the Middle East oil nations belong? Or American Blacks? Or the thin ranks of wealthy South Americans? To divide our globe with artificial geopolitical divisions is an outmoded and limiting way of thinking. People who make such concepts basic to their understanding need liberation.

Are there two worlds today? Surely, this is a more reasonable way to think. As you look around yourself and the world, there's a lot to be said for dividing people into two classes—the oppressed and the oppressors. Marxist ideas have contributed to this way of dividing humanity. But just commonsense and a careful evaluation of power relationships lend credence to this outlook. The rich keep getting richer and the poor keep getting poorer. From 1960 to 1974, the average annual output per person in the industrialized nations rose from $2,768 to $4,550, while the corresponding figure for each of the one billion people in the poorest countries remained the same (even in the face of inflation), namely, $116.

This division is, indeed, an important fact about the planet we inhabit. But it is not the final truth. Oppressed and oppressors do have to live together in one interwoven matrix of humanity. Furthermore, as Paulo Freire points out in *Pedagogy of the Oppressed,*[8] boxed-in people often take on some of the characteristics of their oppressors. They will find it natural to trample other people when they can. In a South American *favella,* or shantytown, men who are themselves cowed by their masters will exact abject submission from their wives if they can. In many cultures (ours included) adults still batter and dominate their children.

Nor are oppressors free of oppression themselves. Perhaps this is closer to the experience of middle-class Americans, who, from a world perspective, are among the oppressor classes. There is no genuine freedom in the posture of those who claim to be superior or those who enjoy conspicuous privileges at the expense of miserable living conditions for other people. Efforts at dominance through power are never totally successful. They lead to degrading actions; they generate insecurity, fear of reprisal or revolution, and feverish efforts to shore up real or imagined weak spots.

Only one-world thinking is truly free. Humanity is one global village on one spaceship earth. Increasingly, our commonsense tells us that; but our Christian faith asserts that as well. Fundamentally every human being is a child of God and one for whom Christ died. Living in Christian freedom means living globally here and now. Exercising our Christian freedom also means living out a vision of that united human society for which we yearn, and toward which God calls the human race.

Fear of the Future

In the previous chapter and thus far in this one, we have been describing the Christian life as it takes shape in response to the way God moves within contemporary history. We have focused upon our own lifestyles as agents of reconciliation or as liberators.

Now let's shift to the question of the church's service—for which lifestyles are but a preparation—to the whole of the modern world. We have stated that it is the church's role to be the connection between its Lord and the needs of the contemporary world. Our descriptions can be brief because they have been anticipated in previous discussions. What does the world need most?

Liberation. Therefore the church's service is liberation—joining God at work in the revolution of rising expectations to bring full freedom to human beings everywhere. But here we ought to be a little more explicit. What forms will this liberation take to fit the world's most pressing needs and to provide the church's most fitting services? We shall point to three. Particularly the first two follow closely from our discussion of global perspectives.

So much of the world today lives in a deep and growing *fear of the future.* Such fear is not new, of course. For many denizens of Western civilization (the First World) and especially for middle-class Americans, today's trends provoke great anxiety about the future of our civilization and our national life. This is tough for Americans because our history has been full of expansionist optimism.

This spreading anxiety takes at least two directions. The one is fear of our own dehumanizing, technological juggernaut. We are afraid that our technological civilization has gotten out of hand and threatens to crush us. New York City becomes a symbol for a great center of our civilization that has become unmanageable and threatens to become unlivable. Pollution, shortages, power emergencies, swollen welfare rolls, vulnerability to modern attack, chronic inflation and unemployment, internal conflicts and outbursts, shrinking tax bases, extreme poverty, a sinking standard of living, the decay of public services, etc.—we feel that the whole thing is going to fall apart. To what will we flee?

The second direction for the rampant fear is those very New Worlds That Are Coming. This great movement for liberation, the widely hailed revolution of rising expectations will leave us behind, or simply sweep us aside. It looks as though the future lies with people who are non-white, non-middle–class, non–Northern Hemisphere, and not a part of Western civilization. They will destroy our affluence, our security, and our cultural advantage. The First World is waning. We have long feared the Second World of communism. Now to join our fear of communism, comes the threat of something vague (the have-nots) called the Third World. The future looks grim; we start to pity our grandchildren.

It is, of course, a serious worldwide problem, if Western civilization and the huge cities of our globe cannot maintain themselves. Let us confess that Christians do not have answers to these mammoth and complex problems.

But Christians do have hope, and they can provide hope as their service to those parts of our world that are in the clutches of fear or despair. We know that fear of the Lord comes first, not fear of change. Nor is our hope based on anything less than the Lord. Ultimately, our commitment is not to Western civilization.

Ultimately, our commitment is not even to the survival of the human race. It is to God's kingdom. This transcendent (beyond this world) reference wards off anxiety and panic, giving us a steady confidence and an enduring hope. Ultimately, we look for a transvaluation of our earthly values and a transformation of the human beings now on this earth.

Yet, we are deeply involved in the issues of life here and now, and we are working for the most humane values within our present societies. This relevant transcendence, this detached involvement, this in-but-not-of posture makes us Christians useful both in what we are enabled to accomplish and as signs of hope to those around us. The confident quality of our lives and the dedicated service in our actions provide encouragement where it is desperately needed. God may even use these modest signs of hope to save (by transformation) this old civilization, if He/She so chooses. But our hope does not depend on that!

The Need for Unity

What does the world need most? In addition to hope for the future, there is an urgent *need for unity.* Not simply the geographical and technological one which already exists. Rather, we need some bond, some unifying force, some recognized and common commitment, a shared culture and language, and a way of recognizing our unity as one fellowship of human beings. Without such a bond, or sense of common investment, we shall tear each other apart. And there is just no question of our power to destroy each other in this generation. That looming threat of destruction can readily be interpreted as God's pressing call to contemporary humanity to move onto a new plane of human unity.

It is as though a large family of orphans has been farmed out for many years, each youngster raised in a different household. Now they have been thrust under one roof again and told to live as a family. Some of the children remember some common family traditions; others do not. The Christians are those few who remember an inspired older Brother whose example has real possibilities for drawing us together again—many others lack that memory or reject that example.

How does unity emerge in this situation? Nobody really knows. But this much can be said, it will take serious and sustained dialogue, with the hope that consensus will emerge.

Christians serve in this sharply pluralistic situation by *committing themselves to the dialogue* and contributing some useful ingredients. Most obviously, a lifestyle of world-consciousness will be quite valuable in rendering this service.

Actually, Americans have a unique experience that, rightly interpreted, could be useful within the world's dialogues. We don't have answers to the pluralism/unity tension, but we have experience and some viable procedures. American Christians can help to interpret that experience.

The word "dialogue" means to talk through. It implies a search for common ground. For Christians it will involve a committed and sensitive reaching out to people who are very different, a persistent effort to understand those others, and a willingness to be changed by the encounter. Worthwhile dialogue is hard work, and costly. It can be a rich Christian service to meet the world's need.

Good dialogue involves witnessing. We shall refine our basic convictions and patiently apply them (and rethink and reapply them) to the problems of the age. We shall do this as a contribution to the public good. But in the public arena our convictions are only tentatively asserted. If our understanding of a human being puts us in opposition to a public policy of abortion, for instance, we should say so with all the persuasiveness we can muster. But we should also be ready to accept a consensus that may go against our interpretation. We should uphold and support the public policy and the laws that derive from it. Of course, our support will involve ongoing criticism and the hope of change.

Christians in America are learning to give up the desire for a Protestant establishment (discussed in chapter 3). Christians worldwide can have no ambition at all for hegemony or dominance. In fact, we are committed to a high degree of pluralism as a very healthy aspect of the modern world. Americans have resisted the image of the melting pot. We are learning to respect minority groups, and we are beginning to accept the "unmeltable ethnics." On the world scene neither Americans nor Christians want one crucible with everyone in it.

In fact, let it be said with emphasis, one grave danger for the upcoming generation is that one person or a coalition will bring unity to the world by dominating with force. This would mean an attempt at worldwide totalitarianism—about the worst thing to be imagined for the cause of civilization, short of total destruction itself.

For the United States we could envision a vegetable soup instead of a melting pot. Probably that is too strong an image for any future world society. A tossed salad with many and diverse ingredients would be better. And the dressing—the unifying ingredient—will be light and delicately applied, but recognizably the ingredient that makes the salad.

Christians will add salt, somewhere deep within the concoction and its preparation. I know that the popular song about "what the world needs now" suggests sweet love. But Christian love is more salt than sugar. If we tried to be sugar poured over every bowl of food, people would react to the sweet taste. Some would be pleased and some displeased, to say nothing of the questionable value as nutriment. But salt disappears in the total dish. It makes a subtle contribution to the whole. Actually, it brings out the distinctive flavor in other ingredients. What better service could we hope to give to the world, in all our dialogues, in all our search for unity?

Social Justice

What does the world need most? Clearly, social justice. A call
for liberation can be very broad, including freedom from fear
and from excessive, destructive pluralism. But the foremost
common-sense understanding for liberation in today's world is *a
demand for social justice.* Simply put, the lay minister and the
Christian movement have no greater imperative than to follow
and *to join God's action in the modern world in behalf of social
justice.* That is our third and most immediately demanding
service as the church in the world.

Identification with the cause of social justice is a touchstone for
our age. It has been the frequent assertion of this volume that the
most significant trend in the modern world is the revolution of
rising expectations, and that God's hand is in that movement.
This drive toward liberation and a greater measure of human
dignity for more people takes, first of all, a drive toward social
justice. Even the newspapers and radios that are propaganda
organs for repressive military dictatorships seek to justiy the
ruling regime in the name of some form of communal justice.

Christians, of course, root their concern for social justice more
deeply—in the biblical viewpoint and obligations to the God
known in Christ Jesus. There is a steady stream of prophecy in
the Old Testament, which comes right through the New
Testament as well. The picture of the abundant life and the
descriptions of peace *(shalom)* always include the whole person
in one's relationships to the groups or social structures in which
that person is embedded. There is even a strong strain of thought
among biblical writers which asserts that God is on the side of the
poor and the oppressed in the struggles and conflicts of human
societies.

In contrast, the Christian church in its visible forms in our day
is widely assumed to be on the side of the established powers of
this world. It certainly looks that way within the patterns of

Western civilization. There are weighty historical reasons for this. Nonetheless, the contrast between the church's institutional life and the biblical mandate for sacrificial service to and identification with the poorest puts the heavy burden of proof upon the Christians. Therefore, it is not only a natural outflow of the Christian life but also a pressing demand for our peculiar ministry to this age that Christians be found in goodly numbers active in the campaigns for social justice throughout the earth.

After all, justice is the social approximation of love. Christian love is outflowing without stint to someone in need. But, with limited energies and resources, Christian parents will cultivate a sense of fairness or justice in the way they handle their children and will seek to inculcate that virtue in those youngsters. In our work world, wherever we have responsibilities that relate to more than one person, we will channel concern with some sense of equal or fair share. In the larger society it is crucial that our love not be capricious, and that it reach out in a just manner to include all those affected. Traditional programs of welfare in the name of Christian service should be paralleled by potent programs of social and political action in the name of Christian love, in an age when the disparity between rich and poor is so marked, when the powerful grow more powerful, and the powerless are made to feel more sharply their oppressed condition.

The real question is this: How do people go about establishing social justice in the world today? This is a tough question, even a discouraging one. One minister put it this way:

> Today people grow fatigued with social controversy. Denominational officials who once thought they were Elijah on the mountaintop now seem persuaded by shrinking budgets to speak their minds like shrinking violets. Consensus will not be achieved on many issues. Practical wisdom knows that the parish church is only rarely an appropriate or an effective structure for social action.[9]

All the more reason, then, why the church needs to realize itself through structures for lay ministry within the great pyramids of our public life. Within these structures there will be need for both a priestly and a prophetic role. We shall need both to comfort the afflicted and to afflict the comfortable. The latter task will be more difficult because true prophetic action usually brings conflict.

In fact, Christians are being called to join the revolutionaries of our day. Not always, not everywhere, but at a conspicuously increasing rate. So many issues are forced upon us for decision and action now. And there is just no way that Christians can forge a convincing lifestyle of world-consciousness or enter into the dialogues seeking world unity or inspire hope among the fearful, without being bold in behalf of social justice. While one group holds another in oppressive serfdom, words like hope and unity and dialogue are empty.

It is as though you are in the middle of a revolution and civil war on an island in the Caribbean. You are an inhabitant of the capital city. The revolutionary forces have come out of the mountains and take over part of the city. From the radio station they proclaim imminent seizure of the centers of power and have declared that a military junta and a radical university professor are now replacing the old dictator who has ruled over a restive people for decades. You know the students are marching with the revolutionaries. Meanwhile, the duly constituted authorities, the police force, the foreign embassies, and most of the symbols of rule remain with the old dictator. Now barricades are going up in the street. You've got to decide quickly which is your side, and then you've got to get with it.

How do we decide? Not simply on the basis of security, not by seeking sanctuary. We do not scuttle behind the best-looking barricade for protection. In a revolution the best-looking barricade can suddenly become empty and useless anyhow. There is no sure sanctuary. Nor are we opportunists looking for a bandwagon on which to climb, seeking the wave of the future in order to ride its crest to glory. We are listening for the call of the Holy Spirit from the world, bidding us join that Spirit at work. We join the freedom-fighters and the justice-seekers even though they provoke conflict and bitter struggle against some of the powers that be. True, God can be on both sides of a civil war, but no one of us can be on both sides. True, Paul said that the "powers that be are ordained of God." But then in Acts the first Christians are called those "who have turned the world upside down." In our day the call is to rapid social change.

In theological circles to speak of the Christian situation in terms of civil war is quite familiar. God is the rightful king of this whole world. He has relied heavily on his deputies or stewards, that is, on human beings. But the deputies have revolted and are now in control, seeking to rule in their own right. This is human sin. The rightful king—living exiled in another land—has instituted his own counter-revolution in the life, death, and resurrection of Jesus Christ. Now we live in the period of civil war, and we Christians are the insurrectionaries, the underground, or rebels, proclaiming the rightful lordship of God in Christ Jesus. We can assert that the pivotal air battle over our island has already been won.

Meanwhile, in our daily tasks we are more like guerilla fighters, engaged in hand-to-hand combat in cellars or out in the surrounding jungle. More than likely we shall end up as part of an underground, in territory controlled and patrolled by the enemy. It seems rather certain that we will not be the commanding officers. We will not be the ones plotting the strategy and calling the shots. That does not mean that we will not be involved and serviceable within the movement.

What kinds of service can we offer? Many kinds, differing widely for different people and circumstances. In general, we can give all kinds of support—money, prayers, volunteer actions—for liberation movements. As stated earlier, if we are not the heroic liberators we can be part of the supply trains, the ground crew, the lifelines. We can seek to bring the concerns of liberation and justice to the attention of those around us who are presently indifferent—consciousness-raising is the phrase for this essential evangelistic task. We can be the ones who apply the canons of justice and liberation to our own immediate place—our job, our neighborhood or block, our congregation, our social club or clan gathering, our school. Nothing is harder than bringing it all home that way!

And then we can add perspective at every point within the campaigns and struggles. We know the decisive victory has been won by Jesus Christ. We know God loves our enemies and the most unlovely among us. We know we are called to be faithful, not necessarily successful. All this gives us a sanity and a balance that are often desperately needed within the social conflicts of our day.

Finally we must ask, because so many Christians keep asking: Can we support violence? Let me summarize this complex question with five comments. (1) No Christian will welcome violence or encourage it. (2) But Christians and everybody else are inevitably involved in violence, from the support of police and soldiers to the use of foods and energy and other products which come to us at the expense of oppressed people who are being violently treated. (3) We cannot withdraw from a violent society; we can and will work to reduce violence. (4) Sometimes efforts to overthrow institutionalized forms of violence lead to more overt forms of violence. Then the basic question becomes that of finding where force is being applied in behalf of genuine justice. (5) We may find ourselves supporting groups who advocate violence to overthrow violent, repressive regimes. We would seek to be a restraining influence. But we are not in a position, for example, to tell African blacks that their drive for a political voice must be entirely nonviolent. We must trust and support Christian leaders on that continent and let them decide on Christian strategy there.

The Violence of a Peacemaker is the title of a book about Dom Helder Camara, Archbishop of Recife and Olinda in Northern Brazil.[10] It is an appropriate title to describe the work and witness of one of the great Christian leaders of our era.

Chapter Eight

Conclusion: Images That Shape Life

The Role of Images

Previous chapters have raised more than forty images for your consideration. These have included well known people (Jesus, Hammarskjöld, King Arthur), common objects used metaphorically (salt, a hedge, pyramids), actions (mountain-climbing, ice-skating), brief stories (a faculty meeting, sharing pencils in school), extended analogies (melting pot, orphans reunited, life in skyscrapers), etc.

A number of our pictures have been biblical ones. The Bible, of course, is full of images, many of which have embedded themselves in the literature and language, as well as the emotions and convictions of millions of people. Most Christian teachers have sought to emulate their Great Teacher who constantly used vivid illustrations, who "did not speak to them without a parable" (Mark 4:34).

Imagery does not take the place of precise theological thought. However, it has much more power to seize and to shape one's imagination, one's convictions, and one's discipleship. A preacher is touching a deep chord, not simply using vivid and familiar references, when she/he refers to pictures like these: eating and drinking together at the table of the Lord, the cup of cold water, Jesus washing the disciples' feet, Pilate washing his hands, "my cup runneth over," "let this cup pass from me"—to refer to only one strain of biblical imagery.

In *Biography as Theology* James Wm. McClendon, Jr., claims that certain images powerfully shape outstanding Christian lives, giving them vision and focus. He also suggests that "the living out of life under the governance of such a vision" provides the best evidence of genuine religious experience for theologians (biography as theology) and also points to authentic biblical faith.

> Our doctrine must be that men of biblical faith are those who find in Scripture what is centrally there—great dominant images, such as those of Kingdom of God, and Israel, and sacrifice, and Son of Man, and who apply them as the makers of Scripture applied them—to themselves.[1]

I do not mean to imply that the biblical events were not unique in their revelatory power, but only that the imagery surrounding those events provides a powerful link to modern Christian living, to provide vision and drive for Christians and to unfold that biblical revelation for other people. That has always been true—witness the way the saints have traditionally evoked biblical parallels as part of the imperative of their lives.

That is especially true today. At the end of chapter 6, I indicated that since this is a secular, two-dimensional age (despite a lot of religiosity), it is those lives that are "lived for others," quietly and helpfully, that God may use to bear witness to the gospel.

In other words, the signs of the faith for a secular age are not primarily internal (eating and drinking at the Lord's table), but they are outreaching signs that are obvious in their social utility (perhaps the cup of cold water or the washing of feet). Interpreting Romano Guardini, McClendon has identified a new kind of saint in this generation, those who take up "the way of practical holiness in daily life." This way is not one of detachment or asceticism but of "self-abandoning obedience to

God's directives just as these are mediated by the secular situation in which one finds oneself."[2] This is an apt description of lay ministry in the weekday world.

Two illustrations McClendon uses are Dag Hammarskjöld and Martin Luther King. Both focus upon the cross, the atonement, and the suffering servant image. Hammarskjöld, who wrote, "In our era, the road to holiness necessarily passes through the world of action," had come to picture himself as a brother to the Brother (Jesus), quite appropriately since loneliness had been Hammarskjöld's great personal trial. That image provided inner strength which enabled him to be brother or servant to all people and peacemaker for the nations. For King, whose cause was black liberation, the Exodus was the central analogy.[3]

The images held up in this book are also outgoing ones that stress lay service in a secular setting with the modern thrust toward freedom. Hammarskjöld could epitomize the former of these and King the latter.

A Swarm of Capitals

Let me summarize the thinking in this volume with generalizations that can themselves be useful images, and potent ones for the shaping of Christian lives.

In a world of great Pyramids within which Conflicts rage, in a world struggling desperately to become One World, the sharpest division is between the Powerful, the rich and resourceful minority, who consciously or unconsciously are oppressors, and the far greater number of people who are hungry, poor, and Powerless. God is on the side of Justice and therefore on the side of the Poor in this conflict, and on the side of One World in that struggle. Furthermore, God's Movement in modern history is best seen in the Revolution of Rising Expectations and the accompanying Liberation Movements, even though the Devil also works within such Causes.

For the Poor, identified with the Third World, God's Movement means Liberation. Or, more likely, during this phase of unusual repression in political and economic life, it means the Hope of a Liberation that is Coming, an anticipation of God's Kingdom itself. There is Hope for other people too, if they can in faith cut themselves free of their earthbound securities, make their Exodus from slavery, and be caught up in God's Movement. For our Human Society there is constant pressure toward Social Justice and a One World fellowship.

For the Church at the End of Christendom, all this means Paratroopers answering the Call to become Pilgrim People of God in joining God's contemporary Movement even with its Revolutions. It means becoming a Disciplined Minority that, like Light or Salt, finds in Service a focus for Dialogue, Justice, and Hope among all human beings.

For the Christian all this means full participation in the Church and in God's modern movement toward Liberation and Unity, by taking up a Lay Ministry in the weekday world. Whether as Supply Trains or far-out Liberators, whether through ordinary associations or through special commitments to the tasks of Revolution and Dialogue, lay people carry Dynamite, Seeds, and Salt into every life circumstance. The Christian will be the embodiment of Love Transparent, a Suffering Servant, both through Christ's Cross and one's own. The Christian will hope to be used by God as a model of Liberation, whether interpreted as seeds planted and giving way to green growth, or as Death giving way to Resurrection.

To this book's forty-plus images, let me add two more in conclusion: an Abrahamic Minority and a bold, beleaguered Bishop, Dom Helder Camara of Recife in Brazil.

Dom Helder Camara

Our group from the United States got there early enough to secure comfortable seats in the pews. People kept coming in.

Some wedged themselves between us, others jammed themselves into the aisles, sitting and standing. Finally, barefooted people of all ages, uniformly miserable in attire, pushed into the pews and sat on our feet—immediately giving us a feel for the situation. The occasion was a service in Recife, Brazil, supporting one of Archbishop Camara's assistants who had been jailed and was assuredly undergoing interrogation/torture at that time.

Vigorous singing was led by another young priest who had been in prison recently. The scripture reading, charged with double meanings in the face of the situation, included passages like: "Rejoice in your hope, be patient in tribulation, be constant in prayer" (Romans 12:12). The intensity was like static electricity. There were several brief speeches. Camara slipped in, wearing his usual black cassock; there was none of the aura or fuss that says "the great man himself has arrived." He spoke in a low voice without histrionics but with rising force. His words (Portuguese and unintelligible to us) had the nourishing effect of bread being handed to the hungry. The service closed with everyone standing, holding hands, and singing the Brazilian equivalent of "We Shall Overcome."

photograph by John Padula

This worship service had no special features. Yet it stands out for me as a great occasion, because it was the first time I participated in a corporate Christian service which was at the same time a public declaration that carried a note of defiance.

Why was this defiance? Because it is dangerous for Brazilians to be too closely identified with an archbishop whom governmental leaders hate. Officials don't dare attack Camara personally—he is too deeply loved by too many people—but they cut off his communication and attack people associated with him, one by one. They call him a communist and a subversive. An American missionary, returning from seventeen days in a Brazilian prison, reported his belief that his captors were really after Camara:

> The most ludicrous thing was one time when I was wired up and receiving shock. (They) were asking about Dom Helder and my connections with him and his connections with me and the Communist party and all that sort of stuff. They were expressing, rabidly, their hatred for him because, as they put it, all he does is go around the world telling lies about Brazil and distorting Brazil's image saying torture is practiced. And while they were saying that, they were giving me electric shock.[4]

The reason for these assaults is that the Archbishop has for years worked patiently and persistently at stirring up hope and efforts toward improvement of life circumstances in the poorest people in one of the poorest regions in Brazil. In other words, consciousness-raising is treason, and interpreting the gospel as encouragement to dignity and self-help is communism.

Camara's identification with humble peasants and shanty-dwellers is genuine and sustained. Tirelessly, throughout his daily round of activities he opens himself to exchange with all kinds of people. He walks around the city and talks with the many people who stop to pick him up. He moved out of the Episcopal Palace, except for office hours, and is available in his small home to a steady flow of neighbors, or to journalists from afar. Short, slight, aging, he nonetheless exhibits amazing energy which quickly becomes a focused interest in the person before him at any moment. I have experienced this personally. In the words of his biographers, "life floods him, flashes from his eyes, his lips, all the dramatic mobility of his countenance, his arms, wrists, fingers, hands always trying with unimaginable energy to make everything bear witness—you, the table, the heavens."[5] Dom Helder never uses the accepted signs of authority, does not even have a crozier. His is the true simplicity of a child. He easily joins himself to artists, intellectuals, or youth groups. He always includes the alienated and the atheists in his thought and speech and visits. His prophetic stance and passion for social justice bring him into the ranks of the demonstrators frequently. He is rightly labeled a modern Don Quixote as he rides forth to speak for the Third World in New York or Dakar, in St. Louis or Berlin. But his tilting is always with the entrenched powers. José De Broucker, in *The Violence of a Peacemaker,* describes him as a priest who combines in himself "all the violence of a prophet with all the subtleties of the politician."[6] Like King and Gandhi, his resistance to the structures is informed, stubborn, and consistently nonviolent.

Dom Helder is politically wise. He can speak compellingly to those in power, as bishops sometimes must. When in 1964 the Brazilian government moved suddenly to the reactionary right and everyone was hunting down communists and leftists, Camara had an opportunity to talk with the new military head of state, whom he had known. When they were alone, Camara said:

> President Branco! Today I woke up rather anxious. Because I discovered that I have a left hand, a left leg, a left half of my body. I am anxious, because I see that today it is very dangerous to be on the left! And now I discover that you, too, President Branco, have a left side. Now really, this is ridiculous![7]

More significantly, Camara's political sagacity takes the form of a steady stream of projects of all kinds that offer some hope for betterment, and dignity for the poor. In the past he has been prominent on radio and television programs, in support of radical lay groups within the Brazilian church, or in sponsoring a variety of activities in adult education and community organization, both nationally and locally. He himself has most frequently pointed to Operation Hope as the epitome of his activist concern for the poor. People struggling to survive while hopelessly mired in wretched poverty are brought together and told that in cooperation there is strength and hope. The result has been a scattering of community cooperatives within Camara's archdiocese, typically focused upon a community center, which he calls "the common dwelling place of people who have taken their destiny into their own hands."[8]

Dom Helder remains from first to last a servant of his church. He has been a leading figure among his fellow bishops, first within Brazil, and—since Vatican II—within South America, seeking to cultivate in the Roman Catholic Church an identification with the poor (and with Lady Poverty) and a sacrificial commitment to social justice. He has steadily offered support and guidance for all kinds of dissident groups while remaining outspoken in his personal loyalty to the Pope. A poetic spirit who often writes little poems in the early morning hours, he once expressed himself with these words:

> So you think that
> because of her weaknesses,
> Christ will forsake her?
> The worse his church and ours
> is marred by our failures,
> the steadier he will support her
> with his tender care.
> He could not deny
> his own body.[9]

The slight figure of the Archbishop of Olinda and Recife is, above all, an international symbol, an inspiring advocate of "the whole family of mankind." It is the inhuman marginalization, he asserts, of so many millions of human beings which makes a mockery of the "family" or One-World understanding of humanity. Let those who are pro-people unite!

Abrahamic Minorities

He tirelessly issues a call, therefore, for the worldwide raising up of "Abrahamic minorities." Here is an image for us too. Abraham has been celebrated through the centuries for his faith and his obedience. Camara stresses that Abraham's faith included a willingness to risk everything and that his obedience meant answering God's call—which sent him out into the desert. In that forelorn place he discovered that *The Desert Is Fertile* (Dom Helder's book title). He learned to hope against hope. "Today, as always," the Archibishop of Recife points out, "humanity is led by minorities who hope against all hope, as did Abraham."[10]

> Put your ear to the ground
> and listen,
> hurried, worried footsteps,
> bitterness, rebellion.
> Hope
> hasn't yet begun.
> Listen again.
> Put out feelers.
> The Lord is there.
> He is far less likely
> to abandon us
> in hardship
> than in times of ease.[11]

Dom Helder proclaims a "marvellous discovery"

that all over the world, among all races, languages, religions, ideologies, there are men and women born to serve their neighbour, ready for any sacrifice if it helps to build at last a really juster and more human world.

They belong in their own environment but they feel themselves to be members of the human family.[12]

It was Abraham who first, under pressure from God, set out from his own limited and comfortable existence and made this marvelous discovery. There are, Camara insists, a minority of people with this vision and world commitment within every institution and place. "Everywhere I go," he notes, "I find minorities with the power for love and justice which could be likened to nuclear energy locked for millions of years in the smallest atoms and waiting to be released." Nor is he speaking only of heroic figures. The average person has a vital part to play. "We should try to form an alliance between him and the frontline fighters."[13]

The point is, get together and get started. If the minorities from each group joined to form a nucleus, they would be irresistible! "If you feel you belong in spirit to the family of Abraham do not wait for permission to act." Start with those brothers and sisters nearest at hand and tackle those instances of obvious injustice nearest to your own place. In the words of the bold, beleaguered bishop,[14]

ABRAHAMIC
MINORITIES
UNITE!

Notes

Chapter One
1. Frederick K. Wentz, ed., *My Job and My Faith* (Nashville: Abingdon Press, 1967), p. 98.

Chapter Three
1. Ralph H. Gabriel, *The Course of American Democratic Faith* (New York: Ronald Press, 1956), pp. 14-25.

Chapter Four
1. William E. Diehl, *Christianity and Real Life* (Philadelphia: Fortress Press, 1976).

2. *Ibid.,* pp. v-vii.

3. *Ibid.,* p. 22.

4. *My Job and My Faith,* pp. 152-54.

5. John R. Mott, *Liberating the Lay Forces of Christianity* (New York: The Macmillan Co., 1932), pp. 44-45.

6. *Ibid.,* pp. 93, underlining added, 42.

7. John Casteel, *Letter to Laymen,* Christian Faith and Life Community in Austin, Texas, April, 1960.

8. For examples, see Diehl, *Christianity and Real Life,* chap. 9, and Frederick K. Wentz, *The Layman's Role Today* (New York: Doubleday & Co., 1963), chap. 12.

9. Address of Laos in Ministry is 231 Madison Avenue, New York, N.Y. 10016. A number of the references to congregations and parachurches in this chapter are drawn from this organization's newsletter, *Monday's Ministers.*

10. Charles Davis in *Downside Review,* October 1963, pp. 307-16.

11. John A. T. Robinson, *The New Reformation?* (Philadelphia, The Westminster Press, 1965), p. 63.

Chapter Five
1. *The Medellin Documents,* published in 1970 by the Latin American Bureau, Division for Latin America, Department of International Affairs, United States Catholic Conference, under the title *The Church in the Present-Day Transformation of Latin America in the Light of the Council,* Vol. II, p. 48.

2. Three of the best known are the Protestant minister, José Miguez Bonino, and the priests, Gustavo Gutierrez and Juan Luis Segundo.

3. José Miguez Bonino, *Doing Theology in a Revolutionary Situation* (Philadelphia: Fortress Press, 1975), pp. 89-90.

4. Ivan Illich, "Why We Must Abolish Schools" in *Ivan Illich: On Education* (Washington, D.C.: Center for Educational Reform Publication, National Student Association, 1969), p. 8, quoted from a paper by Arne Markland.

5. *Ibid.*

6. Gustavo Gutierrez, *A Theology of Liberation* (Maryknoll, N.Y.: Orbis Books, 1973), pp. 36, 37.

7. *Ibid.*

8. Robert McAfee Brown, "Context Affects Content: The Rootedness of All Theology," in *Christianity and Crisis,* July 18, 1977, pp. 170 ff.

Chapter Six

1. John E. Schramm, "Parish as Christian Community," in *Confusion and Hope,* ed. Glenn R. Bucher and Patricia R. Hill (Philadelphia: Fortress Press, 1974), p. 111.

2. Roy Blumhorst, "Answers to Three Questions" (mimeographed sheet from the Center for Creative Ministry, 6325 Camden Street, Oakland, Calif. 94605).

3. Wentz, *My Job and My Faith,* pp. 39-40.

4. The following section appeared in altered form in *The Lutheran,* May 22, 1963.

5. Elizabeth Lodor Merchant, comp., *King Arthur and His Knights* (Philadelphia: John C. Winston, 1927).

6. Charles M. Sheldon, *In His Steps* (Nashville: Broadman Press, 1935).

7. Wentz, *My Job and My Faith,* p. 11-12.

8. *Ibid.,* p. 21.

9. *Ibid.,* pp. 125-26.

10. *Ibid.,* pp. 63-64.

11. *Ibid.,* pp. 74-75.

Chapter Seven

1. *Chicago Daily News,* April 21, 1977, p. 2.

2. Ed Willock, *Ye Gods* (New York: Sheed & Ward, 1948), p. 121.

3. *Ibid.,* p. 123.

4. William E. Diehl, "Sunday to Monday: 180° Turn," *Lutheran Forum,* May, 1977, p. 18.

5. James Scherer, *Global Living Here and Now* (New York: Friendship Press, 1974), p. 11.

6. *Ibid.,* p. 70.

7. David J. Kalke, *Christian Century,* August 17, 1977, p. 722.

8. Paulo Freire, *Pedagogy of the Oppressed* (New York: Herder and Herder, 1971).

9. Royal F. Shepard, Jr., "Manifesto for the New Liberal Church," *Christian Century,* October 6, 1976, p. 839.

10. José De Broucker, *The Violence of a Peacemaker* (Maryknoll, N.Y.: Orbis Books, 1970).

Chapter Eight

1. James Wm. McClendon, Jr., *Biography As Theology* (Nashville, Abingdon, 1974), p. 95, original italics eliminated.
2. *Ibid.,* p. 187.
3. *Ibid.,* pp. 58-59, 89-90.
4. *Lutheran Standard,* December 3, 1974, p. 23.
5. De Broucker, *The Violence,* p. 8.
6. *Ibid.,* p. 47.
7. *Ibid.,* p. 50.
8. *Ibid.,* p. 93.
9. Helder Camara, *The Desert Is Fertile* (Maryknoll, N.Y.: Orbis Books, 1974), p. 41.
10. De Broucker, *The Violence,* p. 59.
11. Camara, *The Desert,* pp. 29-30.
12. *Ibid.,* p. 4.
13. *Ibid.,* pp. 3, 49.
14. *Ibid.,* p. 43, chapter title.